Mary Hunt's

DEBT PROOF
YOUR KIDS

Mary Hunt's

DEBT PROOF YOUR KIDS

"An interesting thing
happened on the way to getting
a financially confident life...
my kids got one too."

MARY HUNT

1948.

Founder and Publisher of *Cheapskate Monthly*™

BROADMAN
&HOLMAN
PUBLISHERS

Nashville, Tennessee

0-8054-1518-1

Published by Broadman & Holman Publishers, Nashville, Tennessee
Editorial team: Vicki Crumpton, Janis Whipple, Kim Overcash
Typesetting: PerfecType, Nashville, Tennessee

Unless otherwise noted, Scripture quotations are from the CEV, the
Contemporary English Version © American Bible Society 1991, 1992, used
by permission; also used are the Holy Bible, New International Version,
© 1973, 1978, 1984 by International Bible Society; NASB,
the New American Standard Bible, © the Lockman Foundation,
1960, 1962, 1963, 1968, 1971, 1972, 1973, 1975, 1977, used by
permission; and KJV, the Holy Bible, King James Version.

Dewey Decimal Classification: 649
Subject Heading: SAVING AND THRIFT/CHILDREN—FINANCE,
PERSONAL/CHILD REARING
Library of Congress Card Catalog Number: 98-34237

Library of Congress Cataloging-in-Publication Data
Hunt, Mary, 1948–
    Debt-proof your kids: how to teach children the skills they need
    to stay out of debt and prosper in the real world / Mary Hunt.
       p. cm.
   ISBN 0-8054-1518-1 (pbk.)
   1. Saving and thrift. 2. Children—Finance, Personal.
   3. Child rearing. I. Title
HQ784.S4H86   1998
    649:1—dc21   217

      12.99

                                       98-34237
                                          CIP

2 3 4 5 6 02 01 00 99 98

DEDICATION

— $\$$ —

To my sons, Jeremy and Josh, in whose lives debt-proofing was conceived, developed, and continues to be tested and found remarkably effective. I love you forever.

Acknowledgments

— $$$ —

I would like to acknowledge and thank several people who have had a profound impact upon my life.

Vicki Crumpton, editor and friend, thanks for your perfect blend of skill and patience. I appreciate all you and your team, Janis Whipple and Kim Overcash, do to make me look good.

Cathy Hollenbeck, assistant and friend, thanks for taking the reins and keeping the *Cheapskate Monthly* office on track and me pointed in the right direction. I depend on you more than you know.

Ken Stephens, Bucky Rosenbaum, Mark Lusk, Joe Questel, and all of my Broadman & Holman family, thanks for your enthusiasm and unwavering support.

Jeremy and Josh, you're the best sons a mom could ever hope to have, and I love you more than you can imagine. Thanks for teaching me enough to fill a book.

Harold, my husband, thanks for walking beside me all these years. It's been a quite a journey, and I can't wait to see what the next twenty-eight years has for us.

TABLE OF CONTENTS
— $💲$ —

Introduction
Read This First!

— $\$$ —

A n interesting thing happened on my way to getting a financial life. My kids got one too.

While our two boys, Jeremy and Josh, were still young, I awoke from a twelve-year-spending coma to discover we were in the fast lane to financial ruin. I had done terribly with money and credit cards. Our situation brought new meaning to the term *debilitating debt.* We were in a horrible jam.

But even worse than the debt was this terrifying thought: What if our kids turn out like me? Were they learning from my behavior that they, too, were entitled to have what they wanted even when they didn't have the money to pay for it? Were they learning to worship money? Did they notice their mom trusting Visa and MasterCard more than she trusted God to take care of our family?

Clearly, I was setting my kids up to become powerless pawns in the hands of an eager credit industry poised to enslave them to a lifetime of debt.

My husband Harold and I had so many hopes and dreams for our children—these two boys we knew God had given to us to care for and then to let go of. Everything He designed them to become was all there at the moment of the gifting. There was nothing we could do to improve on His perfect designs, but if things didn't change we were about to mess them up. Big time.

We had to find a way to teach them the truth about consumer debt and money. They had to learn that if they opened their lives to it, debt could prevent them from reaching their potential. Debt could negatively impact their adult relationships, diminish their options, ruin their futures, and destroy their dreams.

It seemed to me that if we could teach our children not to touch a hot stove, we could train them not to get burned by the lure of credit card debt. If we could train them to look both ways before crossing the street, we could teach them to carefully read the fine print. If we could instill in them the value of delaying gratification, that could become a lifetime behavior.

The following years proved to be remarkable in the Hunt home. I had a lot to learn and a huge financial mess to clean up. And the boys? They learned about personal finance right along with me.

Harold and I designed an aggressive, yet simple, kid-sized financial plan. In a nutshell, we assigned to each of our children a portion of the family's financial resources to manage—an amount commensurate with each son's age, needs, and ability. Yes, we handed over fairly large sums of money to their discretion and control. They had to go through Basic Training. They had rules to obey about giving and saving. They had expenses to cover, decisions to make, and consequences to suffer. Because money management was something real that required lots of responsibility, our boys eagerly learned the fundamentals of personal finance. They learned that to whom much is given, much is required. Sure, they were just kids, but they weren't play-acting—this was the real thing. And these kids rose to the occasion. Wow, did they rise!

If our plan had been a miserable failure, you can be sure you wouldn't be holding this book in your hands. And had I known I would someday tell the story and offer the plan to you, I would've taken notes.

Thankfully, I have something better than notes or lesson plans. I have the living results in Jeremy and Josh. I'm eager to let you get to know them better in the chapters that follow.

If I've learned anything from the stacks of mail I've received over the years, it's this. America's kids, churched and unchurched alike, are leaving home and going into the real world knowing a lot of things. But money management is not one of them.

This is a chilling fact considering the real world is that place where 90 percent of all divorces find their roots in financial disharmony;[1] where personal bankruptcy filings reached an all-time high of 1.3 million in 1997[2] even though it was one of the most robust economic periods of all time; where a $1.27 trillion consumer credit industry[3] is

poised and ready to lure your unsuspecting young adult
into its horrible pit of consumer debt. No doubt about it—
what kids don't know about money *can* hurt them.

As godly parents, we make sure our kids get lots of
Sunday school, church, summer camp, and even private
school. We enroll them in sports and expose them to music
and computers. We dole out wads of cash to make them
good drivers. But a financial learner's permit? Hands-on
money training? Judging from the heart-wrenching letters
I'm receiving from young couples and single parents I can
tell you, it's not happening.

Financial awareness shapes responsible kids. Teaching
kids about money allows them to experience real-life situations and make real decisions and mistakes while within
the safety net of their parents' care.

The debt-proofing process will make the adolescent
years so much happier around your house. That's because
the process builds a child's confidence and problem-solving
ability and makes basic mathematic skills more practical. It
teaches values like honesty, responsibility, generosity, and
hard work. This process of debt-proofing kids is gratifying
for parents because the results are measurable and tangible.

Because money has such universal appeal and understanding, I've found that kids respond to it in similar ways,
regardless of their temperaments or particular natural bents.
Take my kids for instance. You could not find two more
opposite people, unless of course you consider their parents.
Jeremy is gregarious, goal-oriented, excited and, shall we
say, controlling. Josh our procrastinator, on the other hand,

is calm, relaxed, and easy-going. But as different as they are in personality and temperament, when given the opportunity to manage money and make their own decisions, both became very responsible and confident in all areas of their lives—not just finances. Jeremy jumped right in and took control. Josh was less sure in the beginning and asked for advice along the way. But in the end our plan produced the same result even though our subjects were and continue to be very different.

I'm stopping short of saying that teaching your kids about personal finance and the pitfalls of consumer debt will guarantee them lives of ease. I can't promise that, but I will predict that if you make a concerted effort to teach your kids about money and debt, they will walk into an adult financial world with the abilities they need to hold their own.

No matter your level of financial confidence, the amount of debt you may be carrying, or the mistakes you have made in your own life, teaching kids about money management is easy. Even if your own financial house could use a bit of tidying, you can start right away to debt-proof your kids. You will learn in the process.

I introduce this concept of debt-proofing your kids to you as a friend, not an expert. I didn't breeze through the child-rearing years, believe me! Parenting is difficult work and probably the most challenging job I've faced in my life to date. Even though our boys are now adults, they will always be our kids and we their parents, which means we will always be learning. We didn't do everything perfectly by any means, but we did discover some amazing things that I believe will be of tremendous value to you and your family.

And now it's only fair that I warn you: When it comes to consumer debt I am seriously opinionated. And on the topic of children—my own children particularly—I am unspeakably passionate.

My prayer is that by the time you finish the final chapter of this book you will be keenly aware of the danger debt poses to the future of your children. But more than that, you will be ready, willing, and able to prepare them to face that danger as debt-proofed kids. Let's get going!

Note: Throughout this book all references to "debt" should be understood as unsecured consumer debt unless otherwise noted.

Chapter 1
Debt-Proofing: What's It All About?

— $\$$ —

Your kids are fortunate to be growing up in the most progressive and exciting time in all of history. That's the good news. The bad news is the very culture that offers them the world is also perpetrating a lie: *You are entitled to have everything you want even if you don't have the money to pay for it. It's not a problem—just charge it!*

There's a huge consumer credit industry anxious to fund that lie for your kids. They are planning to give your children their very own credit cards—personal passports to the abyss of consumer debt. This is not going to require your permission or approval. Unless you intervene your kids may gladly accept. That could be the beginning of the end of all the hopes and dreams you have for your children's futures.

Do I mean to scare you? You bet I do. I feel like a flag man standing along the highway frantically waving you down. I'm begging you to stop and listen because there's

serious danger ahead. You won't have to turn back, but I
need to show you the detour.

THEY'RE BEING PREPPED

Your children are developing into world-class consumers. They are well on their way to becoming future
debtors. The preparation is going on every day of the week,
nearly every hour of the day. Your children are being
manipulated to think and respond according to the desires
and agenda of the advertising and consumer credit indus-
tries. But the influence is so smooth and subtle I wouldn't
be surprised if you're unaware of it.

If your kids read magazines, go to school, watch television, listen to the radio, know what a fast-food restaurant
is, or have ever been inside a store or supermarket, I can
guarantee they know about entitlement and instant gratification. They probably don't know those words, but they are
learning the behaviors.

(Now before you slam this book closed because of what
you assume is coming, relax. I'm not going to suggest you
throw out the television or ban the mall. Together we're going
to debt-proof your kids, not turn them into isolationists.)

Let me give you an example of consumer manipulation.
Perhaps you are familiar with a campaign of television
commercials for MasterCard International. The ads capitalize on the value of human relationships. They're packed
with emotion—the kind of productions that stir the soul.
Each ad concludes with this message: *There are some*

things money cannot buy—for everything else there's MasterCard. Now think about that for a minute. You and I know that's not really true—MasterCard doesn't provide us with everything money can buy. But the sentiment makes us feel warm and fuzzy about MasterCard.

But what about your children? Take your eight-year-old daughter who, by the way, is the age at which children are very literal. This is what she hears: Everything money can buy is yours when you have MasterCard.

Multiply that kind of message by at least a zillion and you'll begin to comprehend what a child is exposed to in this country before he or she reaches the age of eighteen. Without parents who educate and are role models to the contrary, we really shouldn't be surprised when a teenager finally gets that MasterCard and proceeds to do with it exactly what she's been prepared to do—use it to acquire all those things money can buy.

Here's the bottom line. Your children are being seduced by the consumer credit industry to believe in and fall for the buy-now, pay-later lifestyle. If you do nothing to intervene, statistics indicate your child is headed for a life that will be severely impacted by consumer debt.

THE PROBLEM

I have spent many years analyzing the trouble I got into with consumer debt. What in the world was I thinking? How could I have been so stupid? I've talked with dozens of people who were or still are in the same boat.

I've also read letters from countless others with similar debt-related experiences.

I have discovered three common characteristics in nearly every one of these depressing debt stories and disastrous situations, including my own.

1. Financial ignorance
2. Attitudes of entitlement
3. Availability of credit

Think of this as the recipe for making an explosive. Take a financially ignorant person, add attitudes of entitlement, and expose her or him to the availability of credit. Ka-boom! The result is a situation so lethal it has the potential of interrupting educations, wrecking relationships, ruining marriages, blowing families apart, destroying careers, and preventing joy and happiness.

THE ANTIDOTE

The first step to debt-proofing your kids is to make a conscious decision that you'll do whatever is necessary to teach and train them about money and the role it should play in their lives. Next to their spiritual training, teaching your children the values and life skills they will need to live in the real world is your most important job as a parent. For better or for worse, money is the connective tissue that holds society together. It is not optional. We must have money to live. Your kids will need money to live. The only option you have is whether you will address the issue or simply sit back and hope for the best.

The second step in this debt-proofing process is to learn what you're up against. Our society has odd values about materialism, consumerism, entitlement, credit, debt, and money. If you do nothing to counteract the destructive values the world wants to teach your kids, they are going to pick up the world's view very quickly. In chapters 6 through 8 you will learn what the consumer credit industry has in mind for your kids and why, unless you intervene now, their futures will be in jeopardy.

In chapters 2 through 5 you'll meet my family. Harold and I have been married for twenty-eight years, and we have two children: Jeremy, twenty-four; and Josh, twenty-three. You'll meet Uncle Harvey and learn about the very unconventional family financial plan we developed and attribute to his influence in our lives. You'll find out everything about the plan, how we implemented it, why debt-proofing was actually quite easy—plus you'll get an up-to-the-minute progress report.

Teaching our kids about money by appointing them family money managers improved and enhanced our lives immeasurably. The absence of money conflicts between ourselves and our kids allowed us to really enjoy our lives as a family—especially the adolescent years.

In chapters 9 through 16 you will learn how to develop your own unique debt-proofing plan to:

1. Build financial intelligence;
2. Tear down attitudes of entitlement; and
3. Neutralize the glamour of credit.

That's what debt-proofing is all about. It's a specific plan to accomplish these three goals, and it uses money as the tool.

Ideally your kids are young and you'll begin debt-proofing right away. Sooner is better. But let me assure you that no matter what age your children are, as long as they are under your influence and receiving your financial support, it's not too late. There are steps you can take to play catch-up.

Let me assure you that even if your financial house could use a bit of tidying, you can still debt-proof your kids. Even if you know nothing about personal finance, you will be a wonderful teacher. Only God cares for and loves your kids more than you do. And I believe He picked you specially to train them to reach the full potential for which He created them. Because you love and care for your kids so much, you are the ideal teacher. Thankfully, teaching teaches the teacher.

I've been where you are. I've experienced all of those feelings of inadequacy and personal failure. I know what it feels like to be scared half out of your wits about the enormity and awesomeness of being a parent. And guess what? In spite of ourselves, our fears, and inadequacies, Harold and I debt-proofed our kids.

Let me tell you about it. . . .

Chapter 2
Meet Uncle Harvey

— $\$$ —

I saw Uncle Harvey only three times but I felt as if I had known him all my life. That's because I knew the story.

Uncle Harvey gave each of his four sons a whole year's worth of money at the start of each new year. No weekly allowances, no paying for haircuts, clothes, or school expenses. Uncle Harvey flat-out gave them all the money they would need for the entire year. All at once. In cash.

The ground rules were simple: Everything, beyond food and shelter, that cost money became each boy's own financial responsibility. There was a huge expectation that they would manage their money well. Uncle Harvey's annual caution was, "And if you run out, don't come crying to me."

Uncle Harvey wasn't actually my uncle, but rather my husband Harold's. The significant age difference between Harold and the cousins (Harvey's boys were much older), together with the fact that we lived thousands of miles apart, meant I only *heard* about this family. Everything I knew I learned from relatives. But what I learned, I really liked. This unconventional parenting technique fascinated me.

Reports of how this arrangement panned out were always amusing. As the stories went, one of the boys was quite a skinflint. He refused to spend foolishly and was even reluctant to spend his money on necessities like shoes or clothes, a quirk that brought a bit of embarrassment to his mother, Aunt Rotha.

Another son spent wildly and with reckless abandon. Invariably he had to get a job come February or March. Even though he initially had lots of trouble making his money last, eventually he got the hang of it.

What really impressed me was how Harvey's plan worked equally well with each of his boys. It didn't matter that they had diverse personalities and abilities, that they were as different as day and night, east and west. Harvey and Rotha used money as a tool to train their boys in keeping with each son's individual characteristics, tendencies, and abilities. And their hands-off policy encouraged the boys to become innovative and creative. Each son was compelled to create some kind of financial plan, a plan that fit him uniquely.

I played the scene over and over in my head. It was so fascinating to me how Uncle Harvey, a tall thin man of few words, would call the family together each New Year's day. He would slowly reach into his pocket and pull out a pile of cash. Very deliberately and without a word, he would divide the cash into four piles and look each son straight in the eye as he handed him his annual portion of the family's financial resources. Uncle Harvey was the kind of man who commanded your respect.

Oh, how I wished I could have been a fly on the wall during just one of these uncommon funding events. Everything about it—the passing of values from parent to child, the unspoken demand put on these young boys to reach to the very limits of their abilities, the tough-yet-tender way Uncle Harvey demonstrated how much he cared for and trusted his boys to make wise and thoughtful decisions—always moved me.

And how did it all work out? All four boys became responsible and highly capable businessmen. Each of them married for keeps and to my knowledge, each continues to possess uncommon financial acumen. To me there was only one conclusion to be drawn: Uncle Harvey was on to something.

Harold and I often talked about the amazing Uncle Harvey and what a clever man he was. There was something remarkable about the way his boys were encouraged to reach their maximum potential.

Uncle Harvey was himself a successful businessman, so of course there had to be more to this story than a man showing up once a year to hand money to his kids. He must have been an example from the day they were born. Surely they observed their father's faith, integrity, and business sense in action. When their father spoke they listened—and they learned.

How could anyone not see the association between the end products—four godly, successful men—and the unconventional way they were raised?

I made the connection and carefully tucked it into the back of my mind. I didn't think about it again until many years later when we had two boys of our own.

Chapter 3
What If My Kids Turn Out Like Me?

— $\$$ —

I thought I knew plenty about parenting. Jeremy, born in 1974, and Josh, who completed our family some 17 months later, proved me wrong. Seriously wrong.

I didn't know I could feel such love and care so deeply. I had read about maternal instincts and how one's life changes dramatically upon the birth of children, but nothing could have prepared me for the new level of emotions I experienced.

Without warning some kind of Super Mom-power hit me squarely in the heart. It filled me with amazing resolve: *I will do anything to protect, prepare, and provide for our boys. My children will not experience pain, fear, or want. I will run ahead of them to smooth out all of life's rough spots.* I was smitten and desperately in love with my children.

Caught up in the enormity of my new role as a mother, I didn't notice the way my own childhood had begun oozing into my consciousness.

NOT A TYPICAL CHILD

My parents considered me a difficult child, but not because I was particularly strong-willed or in poor health. I cried all the time and for no apparent reason. Not angry or defiant, I was a child with a broken heart. I spent most of my first seven years weeping. What on earth caused such pain? I couldn't explain it then and I don't know now.

A dark cloud of sadness followed me through my early childhood. My inappropriate fears only complicated the matter. The more I tried to be brave and not cry, the worse my problem became.

I often felt lost. No one knew what to do for me, and that left me to deal with the problem on my own. I hated feeling sad and wanted more than anything to be happy.

At a young age I invented a secret way to make myself happy. I fantasized that I was rich. In the beginning my daydreams were simply a coping mechanism to get through the worst times. Dreaming, however, soon turned to goal-setting. I planned how happy I would be when I grew up and became wealthy. After all, I reasoned, we're poor and I'm sad. If I can be rich, then I'll be happy. While that is terribly flawed thinking for an adult, to a child's mind it made perfect sense.

PLAN TO BE HAPPY

I practiced feeling rich by poring over the Sears catalog. Lists of all the things I would buy became my secret

treasures. I would go up and down the aisles of the neighborhood store mentally filling shopping carts with everything
that suited my fancy. I discovered I could will myself happy.

In time I learned to control my weeping, much to the
relief of my embarrassed family. I found success in school,
loved music, and became a fairly decent pianist. But through
all the years of progress and seasons of growth, the dark
clouds only parted. The sadness would go away for a while,
but my plan did not fade. That I would someday be rich was
always front and center in my mind.

TESTING THE THEORY

I arrived at college with great expectations and mixed
emotions. Scared to death but hopeful, I knew this would
be the beginning of the rest—and the best—of my life. I
planned it that way.

I had spent my entire life preparing for this new chapter.
Convinced that real happiness comes through money and
things, I finally had a chance to test my theory.

With a campus job and a checkbook I could make my
own financial decisions. I could buy what I wanted. When
my wants exceeded my account balance, I learned the meaning of deficit spending through my creative check-writing
antics. If I could spend money, it felt as if I had money.

One happy moment after another I could banish the
recurring sadness quickly and effectively, albeit temporarily.
I felt such freedom and control. In time, my happy days
outnumbered the sad ones and life was good.

Harold and I married soon after I graduated. Neither of us could have imagined how the emotional baggage I brought to the marriage would affect our future.

I created in my mind an image of what our lives would be. Driving a certain type of car, wearing the right clothes, living in a certain kind of home were very important to me. We didn't have the income to support my vision in full. However, if we displayed signs of wealth and leisure, I could fool myself into thinking it was a true reflection.

Always on the lookout for signs of success, I hungered for statements that would confirm I was reaching my childhood goal. It didn't matter where the validation came from—a clerk in a department store was fine. If I could imagine her wishing she could be me instead of having to work behind that counter, I felt some weird sense of satisfaction. To receive a compliment on something I wore or a glance of approval for the car I drove was like a booster shot. Spending flattered, enhanced, and defined me.

Eventually we moved to living the faux life, consuming as if we had a big bank balance. Consumer credit granted us a lifestyle we couldn't afford. Recklessly living beyond our means became our way of life.

OUR NEW LIFE AS PARENTS

Knowing we would become parents for the first time soon, it seemed appropriate we should evaluate where we were and where we planned to go. We did not take lightly the awesome responsibility we would soon accept. Much to my discomfort, our finances were at the top of the list of things we needed to discuss.

For four years I had spent with selfish abandon and no thought for the future. We definitely needed a financial overhaul. But the timing wasn't ideal. Quitting my job dealt a severe blow to our income stream. We had just purchased our first home and that brought new meaning to the matter of household expenses.

Naturally there were things we needed for the new baby. (Little did we know how soon that would be "babies.") In the face of increased expenses, decreased income, and a pregnant woman's out-of-whack hormones, discussing our financial situation was more than I cared to face. So we didn't.

Confident of the safety net we had in available credit, we did what we had done so many times in the past—we pushed the subject to the back burner. We had a more important issue that would soon require our full attention. We would have plenty of time in the future to straighten out our finances.

DOING WHAT COMES NATURALLY

Faced with the overwhelming task of perfectly parenting two of God's creations we did what came naturally. We overindulged them.

From their infancy I found personal satisfaction whenever I pumped everything money and credit could buy into our boys' lives. In some odd way, as I provided and cared for them I was providing and caring for myself. I discovered I could relive my childhood through them. It was my chance to go back and fix things.

Instead of only dreaming of all the things in the catalogs or fantasizing up one aisle and down the other, I could carry through. And since my efforts were not technically for myself but for my children, purchasing became a more noble act. Self-indulgence became self-sacrifice. Who could possibly find fault in these selfless acts of a mother providing for her children?

When I gave Jeremy and Josh what they wanted it meant a double thrill for me. First I enjoyed their pleasure and then I vicariously enjoyed it as I re-created my childhood.

I could give and do for them the things I wanted at their age. If it made them happy, it made me happy. I liked that feeling. I found more pleasure in buying for my kids than for Harold or myself. And when I could surprise them with something they'd not even thought of, it was better than Christmas.

I wanted Jeremy and Josh to have wonderful childhood memories, so I made sure they had everything they wanted, all the things their friends had—even things their friends could only dream of having. They participated in a full range of activities, attended the best schools, played sports, and wore all the right clothes.

The boys' competitions and assignments became *my* challenges. I wanted them to be winners—whether it was the Awana Pinewood Derby match or the Great American's Day speech contest. I made sure our Little League teams had the prize-winning banners and snacks to beat all. I couldn't fix the scores, and that's the only reason we didn't go to the World Series every season.

The sense that we had only one shot at their childhoods at times overwhelmed me. We had to get it right. I didn't care if that meant using credit to achieve success.

Harold would become very agitated when I overspent and increased our debt. But without financial resources how was I to achieve my agenda of giving my children privileged childhoods? My stock justification for overspending on the boys: *Debt is a small price to pay. How could anyone put a price tag on childhood memories?*

SPINNING OUT OF CONTROL

Things began to turn sour as the boys reached school age. What began as a mother gifting her appreciative children had become children expecting too much.

In spite of all I did to please them—in truth I was the one in need of pleasure—we watched in dismay as our adorable children turned into acquisitive ingrates. I worried the day was fast approaching when nothing would satisfy them and more would never be enough, for them or me.

In other areas of life we were diligently passing to our children important values of responsibility, honesty, self-discipline, and faith. But failing so miserably in this matter of personal finance—allowing our children to observe my inappropriate handling of money and credit and all that goes along with that—had the effect of canceling those other important life lessons.

After years of overindulging our boys, there was no way to ignore that things were spinning out of control. The more our kids had, the more they wanted. Demanding attitudes replaced childhood desires. What was cute on toddlers turned ugly on preschoolers. The more we gave, the less they appreciated. Jeremy and Josh felt entitled because they believed their parents had unlimited cash resources. To my shame I had taught them well.

I made sure Jeremy and Josh felt entitled to all the things they wanted but became outraged and embarrassed when they became active participants. I fed my need for material gratification by bringing them surprises and buying them what they wanted at every opportunity. But when the boys greeted me—and everyone who came to the door—demanding, "What did you bring me?!" my reactions did not include the words "cute" and "adorable." How dare these children of mine become so presumptuous?

Birthday party invitations became a battle just waiting to happen. It was nothing for one of the boys to insist on a sixty-dollar toy for the friend's birthday party. A parent-child fight in the toy store aisle is not a pretty sight. But more ugly than the battle (won by the parent by the way) was what I knew it meant. They wanted to be the best liked at the party, to be the most popular, to impress their peers. They wanted everyone to think they were rich. They needed a gift with a big price tag to prove it.

I tried to ignore the conflict I felt.

I Don't Do Money

The Southern California economy was hot in the late 1970s. There was no end in sight for the unprecedented rate our home was appreciating. I didn't know exactly how it worked—I didn't do money. But the growing equity was my justification for living without limit. We'll just pay off everything later, I reasoned. That kind of fuzzy thinking justified reckless spending. It felt good to impress my kids with our bogus lifestyle. I needed them to think we were rich, but more than that, I needed to believe it myself.

When Jeremy was nearly nine and Josh seven, I finally faced our financial reality—credit abuse, debt, and terrible money management had led us on the path to financial ruin. Yet even though we were in a horrible jam we successfully shielded our kids from the sordid details. Harold left his banking career at my pleading and we headed for the greener pastures of self-employment. Not a good idea.

During this horrible season of our lives a terrifying thought kept running through my mind: What if the boys turn out like me? Clearly they had learned from my behavior that they, too, deserved to have what they wanted even when they didn't have the money to pay for it. But were they learning to worship money?

We were active in our church and the boys had spiritual training from their births. They attended Christian schools and thrived in the Awana program that blended Scripture memorization with physical competition. Both boys showed tender hearts toward spiritual matters and their need for a personal relationship with God. But had I interfered by putting money in the center of my life instead of God? Did they notice? Did they overhear their parents arguing about money? Were they feeling the terror that gripped my soul as our family was in danger of imploding?

I didn't like the cold, hard truth, but I knew my children were on their way to living their adult lives as we were—riddled by debt. I was pointing the way and giving them detailed lessons by allowing them to observe and imitate my behavior.

I taught them by example that when you don't have enough money you don't have to stop spending. I used credit to build a bridge between what we made and what we wanted. And when the canyon grew wider? Just build a bigger bridge.

THE BRIDGE COLLAPSES

In 1982 my life crashed at my feet. We lost our business and an avalanche of debt was ready to bury us. I feared I would lose the only things that really mattered—my husband, our kids, and our home. Completely broken, I confessed to God that the manipulation, the scheming, the deceit, and the lying were sin. I begged for His forgiveness and I promised to do anything necessary to pay back all the debt. Determined to change my ways I vowed to find my security in God's promise to provide our needs.

The charade of appearing rich to my kids, to myself, and to the world slowly disappeared in the light of this new reality. I finally stopped living in my financial fantasies and decided to begin making progress in repaying debt, reducing expenses, and living beneath our means.

As I became willing to change, God made changes possible. As we became willing to be good stewards of all God had given to us, He brought amazing opportunities our way.

We were in the beginning stage of what would be a thirteen-year period of financial recovery. Clearly, it was time to make significant changes in the ways we were training our children regarding money and things. We had to stop reacting to their insatiable demands and desires. Those out-of-control attitudes of entitlement I created had to go.

It must have been a confusing time for the boys. While they were not privy to the hideous details of our financial condition, they couldn't help noticing we were saying no more often than yes. Kids are intuitive—they knew I was going through a time of personal growth. Fair or not, things changed as if overnight. We went from spending as if there would be no tomorrow to finding every way possible to not spend money—and without much explanation.

We knew Jeremy and Josh desperately needed to learn the proverbial lessons that "Money doesn't grow on trees" and "What do you think, we're made of money?" But how?

We needed a great plan with an easy-to-follow road map. The kids weren't getting any younger and we had no time to spare.

Chapter 4
Ready, Set, Plan!

— $\$$ —

R emembering Uncle Harvey's money plan was like finding a long lost treasure. It had hope written all over it.

Harold and I didn't recall Harvey's plan in exactly the same way—it had been more than ten years since the subject had even come up. But that didn't matter. We needed the principles, not the details.

Was there any way we could incorporate those principles into a plan for our family? That was the big question. Clearly we couldn't duplicate Harvey's strategy. For starters we didn't have a year's worth of income lying around. Our situation and lives were worlds apart from Uncle Harvey and Aunt Rotha's. We could, however, use Harvey's basic plan as a model to design our own finance plan—a specific strategy that would fit our unique situation. And so in early 1985, with Uncle Harvey as our inspiration, we set out to design a customized financial blueprint for our children.

Over the next few months planning took priority. We made sure our sessions were top secret. We knew the element of surprise would play a key role in the launch. Whatever we came up with, it couldn't be just another blip on the screen of our children's lives. It had to be significant and life-changing.

Harold and I had been through some tough times in the previous years. Our willingness to communicate openly had taken a beating, and we were working diligently to strengthen our relationship. Now as we united our minds in developing a plan, our hearts knit together more tightly because of our intense love for our children and concern for their futures. Our common goal became our common joy.

It took time, but we did eventually come up with a plan that had all the elements necessary for our family and our situation. It was not long or complicated. Our plan was so simple, even a child could fully understand. By design we threw out all references to potential problems. We did not address what would happen if the boys broke the rules or failed to follow the plan. Taking an optimistic approach we agreed that we would add rules or provisions only as necessary. The following was our basic plan:

The Hunt Kid Financial Plan

Mission Statement
1. To develop our children into effective money managers.
2. To educate our children and steer them away from consumer debt in an effort to protect their futures.

3. To gradually turn over to our children the money required for their care and support as members of our family.

4. To trust them to be good stewards of a portion of the family resources.

5. To adapt the financial training of our children so that it is in keeping with their God-given characteristics and tendencies so that when they come to maturity they won't depart from the training they have received.

Commencement Date. Each child will enter the plan on the first day of sixth grade.

Salary. While in the plan, children will receive a monthly "salary" that will become theirs to manage. The amount of salary to be determined by the parents. Salary subject to annual review by parents, or more often as deemed necessary. Salary to be increased on the first day of each new school year commensurate with parental discretion and according to the child's demonstrated ability to be an effective and wise financial manager.

Mandatory Disbursement. Children must give away 10 percent of the total salary. They must save or invest 10 percent in a real bank or other parent-approved investment vehicle. The balance of the monthly salary to be used according to the child's discretion in keeping with our family's values.

Responsibility List. Children will have a list of items and activities the parents will no longer pay for while the child is receiving a monthly salary. The list is subject to review and revision at any time at the parents' sole discretion. Additional items to be added to the list on the first day of each new school year commensurate with the increase in salary.

Hands-off. The parents will not criticize or interfere with the child's management decisions as long the child follows the rules and demonstrates his ability to live and manage his salary according to the family's values.

Each year we would increase the boys' salaries and add more items to their lists. Every year we would release to them greater levels of responsibility. Our intention was that by the senior year in high school, our boys would be managing all of the money they required—everything except the basics of shelter and food consumed while at home. These expenses would include clothing, school, personal hygiene, transportation, dating, sports, and church activities.

Knowing that our job as parents is to take care of and then let go of our children, we would issue them wings one year at a time. Our hope was that real "flying lessons" from a young age would provide the confidence and expertise to take their solo flights from the nest at the appropriate time.

There was nothing magical about our commencement date, the first day of sixth grade. That happened to be the time in Jeremy's life—our first program participant—when we came up with our plan. In hindsight, I now believe age ten or eleven is the ideal time to start such a plan, for reasons we will discuss in later chapters.

We purposely avoided the word "allowance" because it was too familiar. Some of our kids' friends got allowances. We'd given Jeremy and Josh an allowance occasionally but it had no clear meaning. There was no expectation or guidance—and none of us knew when they'd get it again. Quite frankly we didn't want to reeducate something we'd already tried or deal with comparisons to what other families were doing. We wanted something fresh that would grab our kids' interest and command their respect. We wanted our plan to be so unique Jeremy and Josh would sit up and take notice. The term *salary* seemed to fit the bill on all counts.

Deciding how our plan should end was an important detail we failed to address in the beginning. Developing forever-salary-dependent children was not our intent.

The purpose of this plan was to prepare Jeremy and Josh to become self-supportive for life. We had to be careful not to coddle them into the unrealistic expectation that the real world includes free lunch.

After much discussion Harold and I decided our responsibility to support our children financially would continue through the summer following high school graduation. This would allow three months for them to replace their salaries with real jobs or suffer the consequences. If they found jobs before the three months were up they'd still receive their salary. Perhaps the prospect of a double-dip would nudge them toward independence sooner rather than later. Several years later we added the following to our plan:

> *Expiration Date.* Children will graduate from the
> Hunt Kid Financial Plan (HKFP) three months fol-
> lowing high school graduation, at which time their
> salary will cease.

We had no intention of kicking the boys out of the
house when their participation in the HKFP expired, only
that their salary would cease. As family members they
could still live under our roof and eat our food. Beyond
that, they'd be on their own. Hopefully, college would follow.

Designing the basic plan wasn't as difficult as filling
in the details. What would be a fair monthly salary for an
eleven-year-old boy? What level of financial responsibility should we give? Our boys were very different (and
remain so to this day) so would they require customized
plans? What would work for Josh might not work with
Jeremy. We wanted to turn over the maximum amount of
money possible that would be in keeping with the abilities, age, and stage of each boy's life at the time they
would enter the plan. We wanted to stretch their minds
and deliver a clear message of how much we trusted them
to live their lives according to our values and make our
values their own. Whatever amount of money we chose
would have to be enough to last for an entire month but
could not be so much to preclude the necessity for thrift
and careful management. At the same time, I was finally
learning the benefits of living more frugally. It was
becoming more important to us that our kids learn these
lessons much sooner than I had. We leaned heavily on the

truth that kids learn and adapt much more easily than adults.

All the plans in the world couldn't change the fact that we weren't in a financial position to add new expenses to our lives. Our desire was simply to re-direct money we were already spending. For instance, if we gave Jeremy a total of five dollars over the month to play video games in the past, then in the future we would give him the five dollars all at once. Then he could dole it out to himself rather than taking it from us twenty-five cents at a time.

The time to decide on a salary for Jeremy (our first participant) was approaching in just a few months. We needed specific information and our memories weren't very reliable. We weren't expert managers and didn't know where all our money was going.

As an example, let's go back to the infamous video games. I estimated we gave Jeremy two dollars a month for video games. Harold thought it was more. Beyond that very minor expenditure how much did we fork out in a typical month for school expenses and events, entertainment, snacks, stickers, treats, comic books, etc.? We had to start keeping specific spending records. Thankfully, we had a few months before the HKFP launch.

The results startled us to say the least—almost ten dollars for video games in a single month and four bucks to the man in the ice cream truck. Then there were event tickets, various church functions that required money, Sunday school offerings, club dues, manuals and books, treats, stickers, comic books, birthday party gifts, and on and on. Learning how much money we spent on our kids for non-essentials opened our eyes to a new truth.

From the information we compiled, we determined Jeremy's opening salary structure and first-year responsibility list. His salary would be fifty dollars a month for the first year. His responsibility list included optional childhood expenses like video games, snacks, food away from home (unless it was part of a family outing), school lunches (if he decided not to take a sack lunch from home), treats from the ice cream truck, birthday party gifts for friends, comic books (Jeremy was an avid collector), hobbies (he'd developed a rather pricey interest in skateboarding), school supplies, movies, school events, and on and on. We included a "miscellaneous" category on his list to cover anything that might come up from time to time that we would determine to be optional. Kids are very literal. We added this just-in-case provision to keep us from being painted into a corner by a very clever child. We figured that with a monthly salary of fifty dollars, by the time he gave and saved, he would have forty dollars to manage. That seemed just about right.

Our salary plan did not represent a new household expense. It was the money we would have spent on our children anyway. If we gave Jeremy fifty dollars a month salary it wasn't as if we had to come up with an additional fifty dollars each month to fund a new obligation. The truth is we were probably spending more in an average month—we really didn't know for sure because we'd had no reliable accounting system. For years the money had simply dribbled out of our pockets into the hands of store owners and ice cream truck drivers. It "cha-ching"ed its way into video game coin slots one quarter at a time and was handed out bit by bit for school functions, birthday parties, mall trips, and grocery store treats.

Designed to gather the myriad of child-related expenses into one tidy sum, our plan would change the ownership from Mommy and Daddy's money to Jeremy's money and Josh's money. That idea alone had a significant benefit. As long as it was parental funds there was no limit, no apparent end to the resources. Transfering the salary to the boys inherently created budgetary limits.

As citizens of the household both boys did chores commensurate with their age and abilities. We increased their chores as they got older. However, we decided that chores would be separate from the HKFP. If the boys slacked off and didn't do the dishes or empty the trash as required, their salaries would remain intact. Instead, we imposed a citation program. Our goal was to emulate real life. If an adult makes a mistake on the job, the employer doesn't make a salary deduction. Instead the employee must fix the mistake and make sure it doesn't happen again.

We wanted our kids to learn how consequences play out in the real world. Our citations would be similar to speeding tickets. If you break the law, you pay the fine. But you don't lose your salary.

On paper the plan looked great. We had the first salary structure and corresponding expenses in place. We were hopeful. But would it work?

Chapter 5
Our Excellent Adventure

— $\$$ —

O nce implemented, our plan proved to have all the excitement of a poorly designed roller coaster. What started out as a wild ride settled down to something more like a Sunday afternoon drive in the country.

During the weeks before unveiling the plan to the boys, I came down with the equivalent of buyer's remorse. Were the rules too rigid? Were we offering too much too soon? What if "filthy lucre" drove our sons to become greedy little Ebenezer Scrooges? Or what if this crazy idea backfired and did nothing more than fuel the entitlement attitudes they had already begun to exhibit?

Our boys weren't rebellious and they had a healthy respect for our authority. However, we weren't out of the woods when it came to ugly attitudes of entitlement.

In hindsight I know it wasn't their response I feared or the plan I doubted. Harold and I were confident we had a plan that Uncle Harvey would approve. While it wasn't as clear to me then as it is now, my apprehension was due to what this would cost me. This plan required that I begin letting go—not a pleasant thought for an overly controlling parent.

We unveiled the HKFP to the boys a month before Jeremy entered sixth grade. We explained how he would start first and Josh would follow in two years. We presented the HKFP with great fanfare. This was a big deal for our family—the start of an important season of life, a formal rite of passage. We started with a general overview and followed later with the details.

That Jeremy's beginning monthly salary would be fifty dollars—more cash than either boy had ever seen at one time—was the piéce de résistance. We had his attention and that of his little brother, who settled into the role of spectator.

FIRST WE GIVE

We described to Jeremy all the ways he could handle the mandatory giving rule. He could give to a friend whose parents were out of work, a needy person he might meet, a special project at school, the church offering. The decision was completely up to him provided he gave thoughtfully (a good steward takes responsibility), without strings attached (once given he couldn't demand anything in return), and faithfully.

His questions provided perfect teaching moments. Naturally, he wanted to know if we gave 10 percent of our money and to whom. We had great conversations. We explained that God requires us to give back to him part of everything we receive. We, the parents, give our money to God through the church offerings. But Jeremy would have to make his decision based on what he decided was the right thing for him. He should pray and ask God for wisdom about where he should give his money.

We explained that giving money to a guy on the street corner with a will-work-for-food sign would qualify but could be a little risky. Is this guy legitimately needy? Will he use the money wisely? Perhaps a more responsible way to help homeless people would be for him to give his money to the rescue mission because they know the best way to use the money in service to God. Taking responsibility is the mark of a good steward, we told him. Stewards who prove themselves trustworthy receive blessings and rewards. The rest of the lesson is that once you make the decision, you give and then it's hands off. A gift with a string attached is no gift at all.

THEN WE SAVE

Next we presented the mandatory saving rule. Before he spent any of his salary, he had to save 10 percent. Our family now obeys this rule of life: You always save part of everything you get, so you are never broke. Money when saved earns interest, which makes it grow. Interest is money that goes to work for you, and just like seeds you plant in the ground, it grows and produces more money. The word "withdrawal" didn't cross our lips. We must have taught with great authority because Jeremy didn't ask how to get the money out. By inference we told him you save it forever.

We made a trip to the bank in our neighborhood to open a school savings account (a special account for a child where the parent is a co-signer but there are no fees or minimums imposed). We picked up a supply of deposit slips, practiced filling them out, stood in line, and met a teller. We even checked the counter height to make sure our first participant could complete his transactions without assistance.

WITH FREEDOM COMES RESPONSIBILITY

Next came the list. We spent many of our training sessions talking about all the things in our lives—and Jeremy's—that cost money. We went over the responsibility list and how it would grow each year requiring greater accountability. We explained that once he entered the plan, Jeremy would be making his own financial decisions regarding those things on the list.

My memory says Jeremy's first year list included video games, treats from the ice cream truck, all school expenses other than tuition, skateboard paraphernalia, comic books, snacks away from home, gifts for birthday parties, stickers, social events, and related expenses—in short, everything we considered kid-optional and for which we'd given him spending money in the past.

Amazingly, Jeremy never questioned any part of the plan. He welcomed everything we told him about the HKFP and accepted as if it were the law of the land. That to me was confirmation of an important fact: children want boundaries. They crave the security that limits and clear expectations convey.

BOOT CAMP

In the following weeks we explored many different scenarios. "If we go out to eat pizza with friends (a typical family occasion for us), you'll have to remember to bring your own quarters if you intend to play video games." "If you are invited to a friend's birthday party and you choose to attend, you'll be responsible to pay for their gift." (Finally a way to stop those parent-child birthday party gift battles and the ugly taste those wars left in our mouths.)

We discussed at length the consequences of making unwise choices. "If you forget to bring quarters to the pizza parlor Friday night, you won't get to play" or "If you bring too much of your money and go nuts, you won't have any more money for a whole month." "If you choose to buy an expensive gift for a friend's birthday you'll have to say no to other things during the month. The choices you make will directly affect your life."

Jeremy's excitement was contagious to his nine-year-old brother and added to the importance of his impending rite of passage. Surprisingly Josh didn't ask for special treatment. He didn't beg for an early start. He fully accepted that he was younger and his time would come.

Along with the basic rules of the plan, we discussed with Jeremy how Christmas was four months away and he would have to start planning soon if he intended to buy gifts. We also tried to anticipate upcoming birthday parties for which he would need to prepare.

We went over the plan ad nauseam. We role-played, we quizzed, we concocted possible situations he might encounter once he became an official family money manager, and we posed trick questions. We went over the mandatory disbursement rules and drilled him on the characteristics of a good steward. We made charts showing how money grows when exposed to compound interest.

Jeremy's understanding and ability to process this information was amazing. He could respond with creative solutions to any challenge we posed. He knew the plan backward and forward and there was no doubt—this kid was ready!

FIRST PAYDAY

On that first payday Jeremy received his salary in cash—ten five-dollar bills. Just as rehearsed so many times in the preceding months, he put 10 percent into the giving envelope and took off for the bank with the five-dollar savings account deposit. This was about the easiest training we had ever done. He just "got it."

Jeremy knew his exact financial obligations in the coming month. While not a requirement, I suspected he had made lists for how he would manage his newly found source of wealth. We felt great relief and even a bit of pride. After all, fifty dollars represented quite a risk to take on someone so young, so inexperienced.

MELTDOWN

And then it happened. Jeremy hadn't been home from the bank for more than five minutes when he asked to go to the toy store. What?! I panicked momentarily and then calmed down as I realized he must need to comparison shop for his brother's upcoming birthday or get a jump on that Christmas shopping.

We had drilled into Jeremy's head the idea of planning ahead. There was no way he could have selfish motives in mind! Sure, he had been one to feel entitled to anything he wanted, but we had cut him off at the pass. To eliminate attitudes of entitlement was the heart and soul of the HKFP—the reason we had just spent the better part of the summer preparing and training.

To say the trip to Toys R Us was difficult would be to make a gross understatement. I had to bite my tongue to keep from blurting out, "What in the world is this all about, young man?! Just exactly what are you planning to buy? How much money did you bring? Are you sure you remember everything we've talked about? I had a feeling you were too young to trust with this much responsibility. We should have known better. You're the oldest. You have to be a good example to Josh." Internally I lost control. Containing the frustration, disappointment, and anger wasn't easy.

I wish I'd had a video camera. Not only could I have captured this moment for posterity, filming the scene would have provided something constructive to take my mind off what was happening.

I don't know when I've seen such a fixated shopper as Jeremy that day. He was analyzing and comparing, but not for his brother's birthday or to get some early holiday shopping out of the way. Standing there in his favorite aisle—Star Wars—he might as well have been on the front porch of heaven.

We stood in that store for what seemed like an eternity. Harold and I could do little more than shake our heads and hope for the best. We had made a pact that we would not interfere, criticize, or in any way impede Jeremy's decisions on spending the discretionary portion of his salary. How would he learn if we weren't completely hands-off?

I don't recall what it was he bought that day, but it was some large thing he had dreamed of owning. I realize now that he'd been making plans for this day all through basic training. He'd been dreaming of how it would feel to be rich, the same dream I had at his age.

Jeremy's purchase came to $39.92. The kid had 8 cents to his name to last an entire month. I was mortified.

How could we have been so stupid? What did Uncle Harvey know that we didn't? We trusted in our plan to prevent this very thing. Jeremy knew better than that! He knew we had plans to go out for pizza with friends where quarter video games would be the order of the evening. Surely he was old enough to know the difference between a quarter and eight cents. What was he thinking?

My mind was a blur of doubt and disappointment. What should we do? We hadn't discussed the subject of loans (there would be none, that's for sure) so he couldn't be thinking along those lines. How would we ever enforce such a strict austerity program for four long weeks? Eight cents doesn't go very far. Had he blatantly disobeyed? Should we treat this as open defiance? Should we cancel the plan? Tell him he was a failure? Threaten to never trust him again?

The trip home that day was long and miserable—but it paled in comparison to the month that followed.

Harold and I had many long discussions—the kind we'd never had before. We had always controlled the purse strings and in so doing tightly controlled our boys' lives. In the past we had made all the decisions, often to our sons' loud objections. More often than not we would give in and then kick ourselves. We hated feeling like the bad guys when we had to say no. But that wasn't any worse than giving in with a reluctant yes and then regretting once again how we had over-indulged our kids.

After a great deal of discussion, we made the very difficult decision to stick by our plan and keep our mouths shut. We wouldn't mention the purchase either negatively or positively. We also decided to disregard the obvious state of poverty into which Jeremy had placed himself.

During that first month Jeremy gave away the five dollars in the giving envelope (by his choice he did put it in the Sunday school offering). He might have thought about a savings withdrawal but did not mention or act on it. He missed out on many things. He sat while others played video games (a very big deal to him at the time—hardly anyone had home versions then), he missed a birthday party, and he suffered. But not once did he whine or complain.

THIS HURTS ME WORSE THAN YOU

I, on the other hand, was miserable. I've never been big on watching my kids suffer, particularly if there was something I could do to stop it. But this time I had no choice. If our plan was going to have any hope of success I had to get a grip.

With all the attention devoted to Jeremy's financial plight, I failed to notice how much money we *didn't* spend on him during the month I thought would never end. The pain of it all was over quickly, but not the valuable lessons.

SAME SONG, SECOND MONTH

The second month began the same as the first. We gave Jeremy his salary in ten five-dollar bills. He put percent into the giving envelope and took off for the bank with five dollars for savings.

Apparently he'd become used to his self-imposed austerity program because he continued in that mode during the second month. Only the pendulum swung to the other extreme. We couldn't believe it.

As if overnight he matured right there before our very eyes. His frantic need to spend and accumulate was slipping away. A certain calmness and confidence settled in. It was nothing short of amazing.

Jeremy was invited to a birthday party during that second month. Another Toys R Us experience just waiting to happen? Not quite.

Instead of requesting a ride to the toy store, he opted for the local supermarket. I'm sure every grocery store in the country has a rack that holds packages of cheap trinkets like plastic rings or rubber balls. I've always thought of these as disposable party favors—just one step above junk. No doubt Jeremy had viewed that rack from his perch in a shopping cart many years before because he knew exactly where they were. Clearly, he had a plan in mind. How could we fault him since that is exactly what we had been teaching him to do?

The gift he selected for his friend's birthday was—you guessed it—one of these favor-type packages. I stood there feeling the same shock I'd felt the month before as he blew all of his disposable income on himself in one fell swoop. I wanted to scream: "A one-dollar gift for a friend's birthday party? Are you out of your mind? What will everyone think of you? Worse, what will they think of me? You can't do this! This is your friend. You have to spend at least what he spent on you!"

If I had to bite my tongue in the toy store the month before, this time I was drawing blood. Surely the calmness I'd been feeling was the storm's precursor. I wasn't up to this adventure.

But in my most casual of manners I asked Jeremy if this was what he really wanted to give his friend. He explained one dollar was the amount he could afford and that it was a really cool toy.

Everything in me wanted to stop this nonsense immediately. I wanted to take control and get things back to normal. But I couldn't. We'd talked about not giving up if the going got rough, about making difficult choices and then living with the consequences. I knew memories of the party and the chintzy gift would fade in a few days, but these lessons would shape Jeremy's financial future. How could I even think about quitting? To criticize his financial decision would be to stomp on this young seedling whose financial roots were just starting to take hold.

The second month was as spend-free as the previous one had been caution-free. One time during that month when faced with a video game opportunity, Jeremy played two games and stopped. The rest of the time he watched as others fed quarters into the machines. He'd planned to spend only two quarters and that's exactly what he did. No complaints, no whining. Right before our eyes, a quarter, a dime, a five-dollar bill were taking on a whole new meaning for this kid.

Remarkably, changes were going on inside me too. I was beginning to experience something I'd heard but never known first hand: Teaching teaches the teacher. All of us were focusing on spending decisions and the importance of planning and prioritizing. I became more aware of my spending decisions and began looking for even better ways to avoid unnecessary purchases.

Harold and I didn't confront Jeremy about the spending choices he made during those early months. Instead, we found opportunities in the regular flow of life to talk generally with Jeremy about how the choices we make affect our lives. When we make bad choices we have to live with them. Sometimes unwise choices take away options. We used ourselves as examples, sharing with him tidbits from our lives that were appropriate for him to know.

Because Jeremy chose to spend all of his money on himself that first month, he severely limited his options for the rest of the month. The consequences were fairly benign in the larger scope of things, but to an eleven-year-old boy it was devastating—a situation he would never repeat. I don't believe there was any other way we could have taught that lesson except through real life. All the lecturing, role playing, practicing, talking, or modeling could not have accomplished what real life did.

Jeremy had to test the system and then suffer the consequences. Learning this lesson early, while the consequences were minimal and over the safety net of our care, made a lot of sense. Imagine if he had experienced this kind of freedom for the first time away from home, on a college campus, with a five-thousand-dollar spending limit on a credit card with his name on it. One month would have been all the time needed to plunge his life into a downward spiral.

As the months went by our "Jeremy pendulum" settled down to a gentle, consistent ticking one might expect from a finely tuned clock. His insatiable appetite for "stuff" quieted and his spending was well thought out and deliberate.

I'm sure he made an occasional bad choice with his money in the years that followed, but none of us remember. There really was no way he could make any huge mistakes because there was no opportunity for debt and he could never spend all of his money. The plan acted like guard rails to keep him from going over the edge.

HERE COMES JOSH

It was fun to watch younger son Josh observing older brother Jeremy during those first two years. With Josh we continued status quo, keeping the purse strings tightly closed. We would give him a buck or two now and then for spending money but paid for everything as we had in the past. We wanted to retain a clear differentiation between a plan member and a non-member, which was Josh's status. Amazingly this child, who had such difficulty learning and for whom development was a challenge, understood quite well his brother's privileged position of being "on salary."

For two years he was like a kid with his nose pressed against the window of the candy store waiting for it to open. He was content in knowing that on a very special day—the first day of grade six—he too would become a full-fledged family money manager complete with a salary, a HKFP member.

Josh learned more from watching his brother than we could have ever taught him. Practically speaking, he entered the plan the same day Jeremy did, only he sat on the bench. He learned from Jeremy's mistakes and accomplishments and his private comments to me were priceless. "Can you believe Jeremy did that?" or "He did really good this month, huh Mom?"

Not once during those years did Josh complain that he couldn't participate, nor did he ask for us to bend the rules so he could get off the bench and into the game earlier.

Josh's rite of passage occurred on schedule. We made a big deal about the "double feature" of his first day of grade six, but this was such familiar territory it seemed almost anti-climactic. With plenty of time to watch and plan his opening moves, we were eager to watch his action.

Because Josh had shown the tendency to be a bit of a spendthrift in previous years, Harold and I assumed that when his pendulum stopped swinging so wildly, he'd settle down to become our spender son, while Jeremy had become the saver. To our delight and surprise Josh set a very conservative pace from the start and thrived in the structure and expectation of our plan. No questions, no fumbles, no excuses.

There aren't stories to tell of Josh's financial escapades or foolish choices. He took to the program in textbook fashion, just one financially responsible month after another. Yawn.

YEAR AFTER YEAR

On the first day of each school year, salaries were increased and responsibility lists expanded. We kept turning over more and more money plus more and more responsibility to our kids. They thought they were getting these fabulous raises, but in truth we were simply allowing them to hold the money we would have spent on them anyway. If this were a company, we were the executives, delegating fiscal authority over a portion of the company's assets.

As each boy hit the second year we added "clothing upgrades" to their lists. This meant that while we would still pay for their clothes, now there would be spending limits. For example we would pay twenty-five dollars for shoes twice a year. If we found shoes for the less, we benefited from the good deal—we did not rebate the difference to the boy. However, if the boy decided only $195 pump-variety sneakers would do, fine. He had to come up with the $170 difference, also known as an "upgrade." It's amazing how that simple technique can take pump sneakers from nothing-else-will-do to really-kind-of-stupid in about three-and-a-half minutes.

Prior to the advent of the HKFP, Jeremy was bent on a special brand of clothes. In his mind there was no allowable substitute. I'll admit it—I thought it was cute how this little guy was so loyal to a particular brand. Once we added the upgrade feature to the responsibility list, however, brand loyalty lost its glamour.

At some point, shoes were totally added to the responsibility list which moved them into the area of "essentials." Because of the nature of the plan (the boys had full discretion over 80 percent of their salary), this gave them the choice to either buy shoes or not. Don't worry—our boys never went without shoes and neither will yours. They may not have always been the shoes I would have selected, but that doesn't matter now. What matters are the lessons they learned, the parental trust they enjoyed, and the maturity they demonstrated. Sure they made some regrettable choices. But their decisions didn't harm them; they taught them to make better choices the next time. They learned that the cheapest shoes aren't always the most comfortable and if you are patient the better ones do go on sale sooner or later.

Early on, both boys started saving more than 10 percent. Their savings accounts became a significant part of their lives, and they learned by experience that spending is fun but fleeting, while the joy derived from saving goes on and on.

They saved a significant part of their salaries, they saved their birthday money, they saved gifts of money received at other times during the year. When they earned money from odd jobs and summer endeavors, they saved.

When they turned sixteen both boys bought their cars with the money they saved. (We did finally introduce the concept of the savings withdrawal.)

That these kids could accumulate that much money amazed all of us. They proved to themselves from a young age that five dollars here, two dollars there, a little bit today, and some more tomorrow adds up significantly. And the decision whether to spend or save—beyond the mandatory rule—was completely at their discretion. The requirement was to save 10 percent, but many months they saved 80 percent and lived on 10 percent.

According to plan, both boys opened checking accounts in their high school senior years. While we didn't monitor any of their banking activities beyond teaching them how to reconcile their accounts, to date neither Jeremy nor Josh has bounced a check. In fact, neither can imagine how anyone could be that stupid—to write a check for more than they have in the bank.

Both Jeremy and Josh have become checkbook resistant adults—a trait I highly respect. Given my history with checking accounts, I was worried about how they would do with one. Thankfully, both boys prefer to live with cash and write checks only when absolutely necessary.

No News? Good News!

At this point one might expect to read about all the financial mistakes the boys made and how we, their brilliant parents, turned those experiences to lifelong lessons. I'm nearly embarrassed to report that when it came to money, the years were quite uneventful. The plan went as designed. The fact that we had a plan communicated a sense of fairness to the boys. If that's what the plan said, that's what we did. Even though we made adjustments along the way, there wasn't a sense that we were making up the rules as we went along. When there was a question, the plan supplied the answer.

Ah, Adolescence

The teenage years were the best years of all. We were free to enjoy our kids and they us. We didn't experience the parent-child conflicts that arise because of money pressures the way we observed in other families around us. The boys just didn't ask for or expect gas money or funds to cover this school event or that social occasion. They had their salaries to manage. There were no discussions about annual car registrations or who would pay for other expenses they had. Money was simply not an issue.

Just as planned both boys reached maximum salary and maximum responsibility in their high-school senior years. By then they were managing all of their expenses as frugal consumers. They saved far more than they spent and did not demonstrate behaviors of compulsivity. But beyond that they were profoundly responsible, not only with money, but with their lives as a whole. Those were delightful years.

MULTIPLE BENEFITS

While designed to benefit the kids, we now realize how much the HKFP benefited us, their parents. We consistently spent less on our kids than other families with similar circumstances because we had built-in spending controls. Our family's giving was consistent and our savings level was high. The boys' salaries became a fixed monthly expense we could plan on in the same way we could plan on our mortgage payment. We had our spending plan, the boys had theirs. It was a beautiful thing.

Dividing the management of our household income among all members of the family was a brilliant idea. But, of course, we couldn't take credit for it. It did, after all, originate with Uncle Harvey.

Chapter 6
They're Coming After Your Kids

— $\$$ —

They're big, they're powerful, and your kids are in their crosshairs. Credit card companies are desperate for new customers, and they have their big guns pointed at your children.

It was scarcely thirty years ago when everyone paid for almost everything with cash. Remember that? Consumer credit was unheard of.

Early credit cards like Carte Blanche and Diner's Club had a certain snob appeal because only the very elite qualified to have one. For the average person, paying for things with credit was rare—something our parents would have never considered. Back then no homeowner in his right mind would have ever thought of applying for a second mortgage to pay a few bills and treat the family to the vacation of a lifetime.

Consumer credit has changed the way people live. Today credit cards are accepted as payment for everything from groceries to utilities, taxes to charitable donations, postage stamps to automobiles. And where banks used to be careful to make sure a person did not become over-extended with credit limits, nowadays the more debt a person has, the more credit he gets.

In a mere thirty years Americans have gone from carrying virtually no unsecured debt to a whopping $1.27 trillion. If that doesn't take your breath away you have a very strong constitution.

This thirty-year period has seen an unprecedented boom in the consumption of the goods and services that help make our lives easier, and more fun. But it has also created a society that has become nearly addicted to having what it wants now with little thought for how to pay for it.

Credit cards have made it possible for the typical American family to live beyond its means. The average American household owes about eight thousand dollars for credit card charges.[1] Paying only the minimum payment each month keeps more than 70 percent of all cardholders in perma-debt, a state most families have come to accept as normal.

One of the hottest prospective markets for new credit customers is the next generation of spenders—our kids. While the marketing tactics are often subtle, the industry is going after kids with a vengeance. They're counting heavily on a new generation of debtors who will carry on the consumer credit tradition. These marketers are making a serious effort to get children to believe credit cards are good, that it's okay to pay with plastic if you don't have the cash.

America's kids are becoming increasingly accepting of plastic, finding it far more friendly than cash. And why not? Cash makes you think. Plastic is so easy. Kids see their parents living on plastic, so why shouldn't they live that way too?

THEY'RE AFTER YOUR COLLEGE STUDENTS

Years ago when credit card companies saw they were running out of new customers—the adult market was saturated with nearly half a billion credit cards—they began looking for greener pastures. They decided to take a chance on college campuses. The idea was a bit risky, after all— who ever heard of unemployed teenagers being able to qualify for credit?

To their amazement and fiscal joy not only was the grass on the other side greener, college campuses turned out to be pure gold.

Credit card company reps have now become permanent college fixtures. For years they've been harvesting fat profits, picking up new customers just as quickly as students can register and get into the swing of college life.

These days step onto any college campus and you're likely to see representatives from the big credit card companies seated at tables in the class registration lines. Business is so hot, they vie for the attention of possible new customers. They offer tempting incentives in exchange for just filling out an application—everything from a free pizza to a first-class upgrade on your next flight home.

It's not at all unusual for credit card applications to find their way under college dormitory doors and for credit card companies to offer fund-raising programs to sororities and fraternities in the form of cash referral fees. All the fund-raising committee has to do is produce completed credit card applications.

One sorority sister told me her house gets five dollars for every application they turn into the company's campus representative. "Why should we care?" my informant giggled. "All we have to do is get lots of people to fill out the applications. No one really expects to get a card, but if they do they don't have to use it. It's a really cool way for us to raise lots of money for our house." Truth is, in the collegiate world everyone who fills out an application gets a card complete with an attractive spending limit.

While the invasion of the credit card companies is far more visible on the larger secular campuses, the smaller Christian colleges are certainly not exempt. Even on those campuses too small to warrant a representative, student mailboxes are stuffed to capacity with pre-approved applications and plenty of tempting offers. I spoke with the dean of students of a prestigious private university who reported they don't allow credit card companies to set up shop. However, they cannot censor the U.S. Mail, and so the credit card companies simply flood the campus with their pre-approved applications in this alternative way.

On many campuses large and small credit card companies provide—at no charge, of course—shopping bags to the campus bookstore cleverly pre-inserted with credit card applications. Amazingly, even the most reluctant of bookstore managers finds it difficult to turn down such a "lovely gesture"—free bags!

Check out this new card "invitation" that showed up in the mailbox of Kelly, a young college-bound Floridian. I hope you're sitting down.

Free from parental rule at last! Now all you need is money, Cha-Ching! (envelope copy). Inside is a lengthy, convincing marketing piece that reads in part, *Getting the credit you need to get through college is easier than you'd think. In fact, it's almost a no-brainer. Just send in the invitation above or give us a call. If you qualify, the Associates Visa card will be in your mailbox before you know it. . . . Get 3 percent cash back on everything you buy. Just imagine, 3 percent cash back on living expenses . . . text books . . . everything you buy with your Associates Visa including pizza! How cool is that? All you have to do is carry a balance from statement to statement and keep your account in good standing and you can get 3 percent cash back on all your net purchases. Just think how much college costs these days, then figure out how much a 3 percent rebate would add up to. That's some serious cash![2]*

Who but a credit card company would advise a young student to carry a balance from month to month? At this card's annual interest rate of 17.99 percent, the cost of this "deal" is still 15 percent—a hefty rate. By the way, the fine print sheds a little light on that 3 percent rebate that's supposed to be so terrific. The maximum Kelly could possibly earn in a year is just one hundred dollars, which is subject to all kinds of conditions and exclusions including: *The terms and conditions of this rebate program may be changed or canceled at any time and for any reason.*[3] In other words, many purchases might not qualify for this over-rated rebate.

I'm happy to report that Kelly round-filed this offer, but if she'd fallen for it she would have had to charge thirty-three hundred dollars in qualifying purchases (a nebulous term without clear explanation on the application) and pay 17.99 percent interest on the revolving balance to get that one-hundred-dollar annual rebate. I would hardly call that "some serious cash." But some serious debt? Oh, yes!

Often credit card solicitations come with emotionally-packed messages. Jeremy received his first one in the spring of his senior year of high school. It read something like this: *You're going to college, you'll be away from home for the first time. You'll experience all kinds of new things. Some will be fun and exciting, but chances are you will encounter dangers like car trouble or other emergencies. There will be books and basic living essentials. Your parents won't be there to help. Let us be there to take care of all these unexpected expenses.*

Clearly, this solicitation was designed to move the terrified college-bound student to action with a one-size-fits-all solution for grown-up situations. I can understand how a financially ignorant, frightened teen could fall for this false notion that credit is the antidote for all of life's curveballs.

Tahira K. Hira, a professor of family finance at Iowa State University, conducted a survey of college students and found that 76 percent of those surveyed held three or more credit cards while 40 percent had six or more.[4] The Nellie Mae Fund for Education[5] shows for undergraduate college students the average available credit limit is $6,122 while the graduate student's weighs in at $15,000.

You might wonder how credit card companies can possibly justify extending that kind of credit to unemployed students. They play the odds. They know that most college students have parents or other family supporting them in some way. They bank on the fact that most parents, no matter how angry or disappointed, will come to the aid of their children when they get into trouble. And they have also discovered that students who have been "bailed out" by Mom and Dad are excellent risks for new cards because if parents will rescue them once, they'll do it at least two times.

There's lots of competition these days between credit card companies, and that's what drives the marketing campaigns. According to David Sandor of Visa USA, "Card companies want to establish a long-term relationship. They want to be the card that gets carried in the wallet for many years."[6]

One Loyola Marymount student I met several years ago had a story that sent chills up my spine. Seems he was fairly impressed with his ability to get credit cards. He had barely unpacked his bags at school before he started filling out the credit card applications. He got plenty—seven cards in all.

Before the second semester of his freshman year he had maxed them out to the tune of twenty-five thousand dollars—in less than five months. He bought designer clothes, stereo and electronic equipment, and computers, plus all the fancy meals and concerts he and his friends could possibly endure.

His high living gained him more friends than he knew what to do with. But did he worry? Of course not. He knew his parents would eventually find out, get really mad, and then get over it. He was right. They did find out. And they got really mad, but they didn't get over it. And they didn't bail him out.

He had no choice but to drop out of school and give up his scholarship. By the time I met him on the set of a talk show he'd been working full time for quite a while. He said he hoped to go back to school someday when he got the credit cards paid off and his life together.

Maureen wrote, "When I went to college I couldn't believe all the credit card applications in my mail box. I even got a gold card with a seven-thousand-dollar limit. I charged it to the limit in a matter of months. . . ."[7]

Like Maureen, most teens have never learned the dangers of unsecured credit. They leave home financially ignorant, clueless how credit cards work. So when they find out they can break free from parental rule by helping themselves to all they would like from the campus credit-card smorgasbord, they comply willingly. Conventional thinking makes the attractive spending limits look like "free money" and work like "free money," so why not?

Cyd recalls how the myth of free money impacted her life: "My first credit card arrived just days after my twentieth birthday. I was so delighted. Getting a card was so easy. I felt so grown up—no longer a teenager. I was living in an apartment and now had the power to go shopping whenever I wanted. I could finally get some decent clothes for work, finish furnishing our apartment, and on and on. Never mind the fact I had to take a second part-time job to afford my share of the expenses and quit college so I'd have time for my two jobs.

"My Visa led to many store credit cards and oh, so much more spending power. I couldn't believe that I could get so much (a two-hundred-dollar spending limit on a store card) for so little (only ten dollars a month . . . that's all?). Adulthood was wonderful."[8]

The pervasive attitude among college students when it comes to credit cards is *spend now, worry later.* Their futures look rosy and immature wisdom says, *When I get out of school I'll get a great job and just pay it all back really fast.* Of course that's exactly the way the credit card companies want them to think.

That's what Kay believed. "I'm twenty-three years old and currently my husband and I are twenty-five thousand dollars in debt not including our mortgage. . . . I went off to college and one by one the credit card offers poured into my mailbox. I applied for several and of course received them all.

"By the time I got out of college I had seven cards and twenty thousand dollars' worth of debt. That's more than I paid for my entire college education. I bought stereos, TVs, clothes, food, a computer, furniture—all the things I thought I needed. I figured I would pay it all off when I graduated and got a good job.

"Well, today I have graduated and I have a good job but my entire check is currently going to pay off my debt. Even with an aggressive written repayment plan, it's still going to take over three years to get out from under this horrible load of debt. We want desperately to start a family but we've had to put that dream on hold because of the debt.

"It would be easy to blame my parents for my problems because they never taught me how to manage money. But the truth is they didn't know either. They often got themselves into impossible situations with consumer debt and had to be rescued by relatives. Never once was I warned about the dangers of credit or taught how to save, give, invest, and manage my money."[9]

When students graduate from college, reality sets in. Their first assignment as an adult is to figure out how they're going to repay their student loans, juggle huge credit card debts, and cover "incidentals" like rent and transportation.

Unlike any generation before, those coming out of college nowadays aren't simply broke. They're in the hole with significant debt and ruined credit ratings. What a way to start out!

Consider this single paragraph letter received from one Texas Tech student. "I ran up seventeen thousand dollars in debt by my junior year, dropped out of college, and filed for bankruptcy." Tragic.

Not all students get so mired in credit card debt that they must drop out of school. But current trends suggest that those students who overextend themselves with credit card and student loan debt during their college years may be setting themselves up for failure when they graduate.

THEY'RE AFTER YOUR HIGH SCHOOLERS

High school? No way!

That was my reaction when I began getting letters from readers of *Cheapskate Monthly* telling me their high school kids were getting credit card applications in the mail. I was skeptical. Somehow a kid's name was mixed up with the parent's. It had to be a mistake.

Then I started researching exactly what's going on. Folks, it's not a mistake. It's absolutely true. The credit card companies are on the prowl again, desperate for new feeding grounds.

First, they went to the college campuses and now they've expanded their sights to a generation of teens. Some major credit card companies will give a minor student a credit card without a cosigner or evidence of income. Only one state, Illinois, has a law that bans giving credit cards to minors without parental consent. High school students can get a credit card in their name with a five-hundred-dollar spending limit.

These companies don't reach high schoolers through television, radio, or print advertising. That would be too blatant. It would likely cause a huge negative outpouring from parents. So credit card issuers depend mostly on low-key, direct mail to get at high school students—particularly college bound seniors. But sometimes they target even younger, as in the case of Ryan.

"When my son Ryan was a seventeen-year-old high school sophomore he received a credit card from a local department store—without parental consent or knowledge. He became obsessed with credit and began applying for bank cards, gas cards, department store cards, whatever he could get, on his own and without my knowledge.

"When he began dating it seemed he was always on the run. It was then I discovered in his room a Visa bill literally two pages long with charges he had made in one month totaling over one thousand dollars. He went crazy charging flowers, restaurant meals, gasoline, and cash advances.

"The strain on my relationship with Ryan was overwhelming. I was a desperate mother in panic. My son hadn't even begun his life and was already destroying it. The arguments we had were horrible; I was losing my son. I tried talking, begging—anything to make him wake up. My child hated me and felt he had no privacy. He started hiding bills from me so I wouldn't know what he was doing. We didn't speak. How could this be happening? This was the last thing I thought I would deal with when my son was in high school.

"I watched Ryan go from a fun-loving, carefree high school student to a hard-working child under extreme pressure. Summer vacations meant working two jobs and no time for fun. He had to give up football, a sport he loved and at which he excelled. He was the star on the team but had to drop out because he had so many debts to pay. His precious high school years consisted of work and school.

"The school became concerned when Ryan's grades dropped drastically. He'd taken on more than he could handle. I can't tell you what all of this has done to me, the tears I've shed and the helplessness I've felt. Ryan is my only child and I've always wanted the best for him. To stand by helplessly watching your son's life being destroyed is the worst thing a parent can go through.

"I tried calling the companies but it did no good. They wouldn't even speak to me about Ryan's accounts even though he was a minor. Ryan has lost the best years of his childhood working to pay off his debts.

"His grandmother and I felt he was doing his best and we couldn't stand to see him work so hard plus try to do well in school. We decided to pay off his debts just before he began his senior year. No sooner were the debts paid, he turned around and charged his cards right back up and went after more cards. I felt like I was going crazy. How could he do this again?

"Ryan would like to apply for college but doesn't have the grades or the sports records he needs to get a scholarship. He sacrificed everything for the debt and he will never be able to go back and make up those years."[10]

You're probably wondering, as I did, how these companies get our kids' addresses. Surprisingly, the names and addresses of high schoolers—your minor children—are public information. One firm[11] says it has a data base made up of eight million current high schoolers. They claim they can provide the name, address, and median family income by zip code for about 90 percent of all the high school seniors in the nation.

Financially ignorant kids see a credit card of their own as a ticket to freedom, a passport to adulthood. Kids thrive on being trusted and that's exactly the message they get when a big company sends an approved credit card application in their name. Give a kid respect and trust, and you'll have a child who feels significant. I must say these companies are smart.

High schoolers who lack knowledge of personal finance, which is nearly all of them, can't believe it when they're offered their own credit card with a five-hundred-dollar spending limit. Five hundred dollars is more money than most kids have ever seen at one time.

Without a strong foundation of financial information and hands-on experience, they usually go nuts. They see it as the end of parental control, a license to spend without restraint.

If you think your kids are safe because you'll refuse to cosign and that they could never get a credit card without a job anyway, think again. These companies are slick. They know that while your innocent college freshman or college-bound high school senior doesn't have a job now, he's likely to have one someday. They also know that if they can hook youngsters early, they'll have them for fifteen years or more (the known loyalty rate on a first credit card[12]).

Normally, one would need a steady job, a history of paying bills, or at the very least a cosigner, but not when it comes to snagging a new young customer. All credit-issuing standards that relate to adults are waived when it comes to students.

Sharon wrote: "Our children grew up having everything they could possibly want. We made a sizable income and could afford to live well.

"Our oldest daughter was quite a go-getter. In high school she was elected student body president and the head of every club she joined. We were very proud of her leadership qualities. We bought her a nice car and she always had unlimited spending money. While she was still in high school it came—her first credit card application. She really wanted it and our thought was what can it hurt? It's only a $500 limit. She'll learn.

"When she got to college the pre-approved applications started filling her mailbox. Within just a few weeks she had a total of five credit cards. We had no idea.

"She maxed that first card and came crying for us to help. It was only five hundred dollars so we paid it off. She went back to school and began spending like crazy—going to concerts, eating out, [buying] a cell phone, new clothes, and crying to us again of her horrible dilemma. Again we paid her debts but this time is was a thousand dollars. We begged her not to repeat.

"During that first semester she got mixed up with a pyramid multi-level marketing organization. She was totally obsessed with money, fixated on becoming a millionaire. Her grades went from As to Ds while she was spending like crazy.

"She dropped out of college in the spring of her freshman year. She came to us with her now fifteen thousand dollars' worth of credit card balances. To her utter shock and dismay we finally woke up and said no.

"She went to work making seven dollars an hour and within a very short time married. Our very bright daughter was capable and had every possibility of going places. It breaks my heart that her dream of medical school is gone."[13]

Paula tells her story of getting involved with credit while in high school: "I left home and started college right out of high school and the credit card offers came right away. I had a great credit report because at age sixteen my mom gave me my very own credit card to use freely. I had no limitations or boundaries at all. She always paid the balance.

"I went to college thinking I would have no trouble being on my own. While the other students were getting credit cards with five-hundred-dollar limits, mine were twenty-five hundred to five thousand dollars each. It took only two years for me to be deeply in credit card and student loan debt.

"I was still at school and my mother knew nothing of my mess until creditors started calling her. I was stunned when she called to tell me she was no longer willing to bail me out. I had no choice but to move home, enroll in night school, and work my fingers to the bone to repay my debts. It took a long time and a miserable time it was. I didn't go out with friends, buy clothes, or anything. Eventually I paid it all back but what a difficult lesson I had to learn."[14]

THEY'RE AFTER YOUR YOUNGSTERS

You probably think you've reached the comedy portion of this chapter, that I'm only kidding that the credit card industry is interested in capturing the attention of your school-aged kids. Even your toddlers. It's not a joke, folks. I'm serious.

The consumer credit industry won't be contacting your little ones through the mail. They know little kids can't read. But they know what all kids love. They've managed to make toys an inroad of choice to familiarize even the youngest members of your family with the idea of credit.

One company offers Kiddee Credit Cards, priced at only three dollars for twelve dozen cards. Your very young children can play all kinds of charging games. These cards are replicas of all the majors plus every department store and restaurant you can imagine. The very presence of this toy in a child's life makes living on credit as ordinary as making a pie in a toy oven or rocking a dolly to sleep. It plants the seed of acceptance and normality.

I'm still shaking my head over Cool Shoppin' Barbie®, and her realistic Playset. It comes complete with a tiny MasterCard that Barbie holds in her hand, a cash register, and a credit card reader that chirps "Thank You" and "Credit Approved!"[15]

Just in time for Christmas 1997, the Store of Knowledge chain of stores, tied to television's Public Broadcasting System, unveiled its alternatives for parents who have had it with violent video games and grinning fashion dolls. Most would assume that such an endorsement from PBS would have our children's best interests in mind. As far as I'm concerned they should have looked a bit farther.

At the top of the year's list was the Calculator Cash Register. Intended for children ages three and up, the solar-powered toy includes a toy credit card and features realistic sound effects. Of all the toys PBS presented to their test group of youngsters in an effort to determine the top ten, the cash register with the pretend Citibank credit card was the most popular.

All three of these toys, with just a tiny tweak, could be terrific teaching tools for kids. The Kiddee Credit Cards could be Kiddee KASH—realistic currency. Cool Shoppin' Barbie could carry miniature wads of CASH and her little cash register could chirp "Cash Sale! Congratulations, you're a smart shopper!" The solar-powered cash register could dump the credit card and contain just—imagine this—CASH!

Sadly, these toys send a message to children that credit cards are good and should be as much a part of their lives as cars, trucks, and baby dolls.

Not long ago I was standing in a checkout line behind a young woman and her daughter who appeared to be about six years old. The lady put all of her purchases on the counter, and the sales clerk inquired as to the method of payment. The woman looked adoringly at the child who was carrying a small plastic toy wallet and encouraged her to answer the question. Without a word the little girl opened the wallet to produce a real Visa card which she handed to the clerk. The mother beamed as she handed the card back to her daughter so she could "take good care of it until we get to the next store."

I was mortified, and if you know me, you'll be surprised to know I didn't say a word. I even turned the other way knowing I couldn't hide my bewilderment. There was a child who will be grow up assuming plastic is the way to pay for all the things she wants.

THEY'RE SHOWING UP IN THE CLASSROOM

Personal finance is not a widely mandated subject in schools these days. Twenty-six states require consumer education but only fourteen of those have a personal finance element. Most school districts simply have no funding available for curriculum—the perfect situation for the credit card companies to slip their biased materials into the classrooms of America. MasterCard, Visa, and Citibank all provide free materials, many of which, in my opinion, give bad advice to kids.

Visa, in their "Visa's Choices & Decisions" curriculum states that it's okay to spend up to 20 percent of your net income on consumer debt. MasterCard International, in its booklet, "Kids, Cash, Plastic, and You" cosponsored by the U.S. Office of Consumer Affairs (your tax-dollars at work), doesn't mention a word about paying off your credit card balance in full every month. Instead it advises, "Credit card balances can be paid off in installments over many months, or even years. . . . It is important to make timely payments."[16]

Citibank, in its booklet, "Money Matters for Young Adults," warns that credit is the way of life in America, and if you cannot get credit on your own, you need to get a cosigner. This publication also advises to keep credit card indebtedness under 20 percent of household income.

For the most part, the personal finance materials available in schools today are compliments of companies that have a glaring conflict of interest. They are looking to influence and coerce the minds of youngsters to accept consumer debt as the all-American way of life. By all indications and most regrettably, it's working quite well.

Consumer debt is one of the biggest killers of relationships, dreams, futures, and happiness. Over and over I've heard the stories of how it started very innocently—usually in college or during the first years of marriage. While the circumstances are all different, the same theme comes through loud and clear: *I had no idea what I was doing. I thought it was okay because they approved me. I didn't intend to go nuts. We got married and because of our student loans and credit card debts we fought all the time and now he's gone.*

Here's a perfect example excerpted from a letter that washed up on my desk not long ago: "I am twenty-two and my husband is twenty-three. We are sixty thousand dollars in credit card debt. I obtained my first credit card upon entering college and faithfully paid the entire balance each month until we got married.

"My husband received his first card at age fourteen when his mother applied in his name in an attempt to get new credit after a divorce destroyed her credit rating.

"His mother paid his balance, maintained his checkbook, and mostly took care of all the financial responsibilities. When he came to college he struggled with money. He didn't know so many credit cards existed and accepted every one.

"We graduated, quadrupled our income, and quadrupled our spending, of course. Then our student loans came due. Things became tight overnight but we still had plenty of money to cover the bills.

"My husband began seeing me as controlling and restrictive with money, not wise and trustworthy as I thought he should. I wanted us to live on a budget and start repaying debt quickly.

"Just a few weeks ago he asked me for a divorce. I had no idea he believed that was our only alternative.

"I know that money is not the only source of our problems, but how we spend it illuminates the differences in how we believe and conduct our lives. For my husband money represents freedom, control, and the right to live his life the way he chooses."[17]

Everything you've read so far in this chapter is the bad news. It's the ugly truth of what's out there waiting for your kids. Now here's the good news—you can intervene. Your kids, no matter their abilities, tendencies, or characteristics, can learn to say no to credit card offers. I believe with all my heart that if kids learn the truth and the dangers of debt early in their lives, potential harm can be prevented.

Please hear me. There's a horrible stalker out there waiting for your kids. As things stand right now your children are in great peril. They are being conditioned to believe that credit cards are the way to have everything they want, and that carrying revolving debt is the way to live. But you can change that—you can do something about it.

It's not reasonable to think we can stop this stalker—the consumer credit industry. Even if there were reasonable solutions, we don't have time to wait for new legislation, to organize massive boycotts, or in some other way try to slay the dragon.

What is reasonable is that we can educate our kids. This stalker is only as strong as his prey is weak. Ignorance will keep your kids weak, but knowledge will fill them with power. If you teach children the truth about consumer credit and how to make wise financial decisions, their lives will be impenetrable. You will have equipped them with a protective coating that's stronger than the attacks of the stalker.

A current print advertisement comes to mind: A beautiful woodpecker has decided to peck not on a tree but on a wall made of a new synthetic wallcovering material. The wall shows no damage whatsoever while the woodpecker's beak is accordion-pleated. It's a funny picture and tells the story without a word. The point is clear: No one set out to destroy the woodpecker, only to strengthen the target so the woodpecker could do it no harm.

Perhaps you feel inadequate to teach your kids about debt and money management because you've made a mess of your finances. Maybe you're really blew it during college and now you're paying for it. Don't let that happen to your kids. Tell them what happened to you. Tell them about the people in this book. Tell them about me, about my boys. Tell them about Sharon's daughter who threw away her dream to become a doctor—all for a stupid credit card with her name on it.

Chapter 7
Future Debtors of America

— $\$$ —

T hey're armed and dangerous. The next generation of adults—our kids—wield tremendous economic power but lack financial knowledge. If that's not scary enough, statistics indicate this generation will make more consumer decisions than any generation before.

THEY HAVE ECONOMIC POWER

Kids in the age-five-through-fourteen category are of great importance to the marketing industry, not only because they spend a lot of money themselves (one poll reveals that by age twenty the average kid in this country has already received thirty-three thousand dollars in income and gifts[1]) but because of the significant influence they have over what their parents spend on them.

In 1996 this demographic group of kiddy consumers spent $24.4 billion on themselves and influenced the way their parents spent another $117 billion on them, an amount expected to reach $211 billion by 2001.

Additionally, this group of kids influences the way their parents spend $400 billion annually on things for the household like groceries, cars, computers, televisions, and where to go on vacation. Parents rely heavily on their kids to be their resident consumer experts.[2]

Today's teens, the largest group of teenagers ever in American history, also have tremendous economic power. First, they have an average *weekly* income of $70—more than $108 billion a year of which in 1996 they spent $84 billion on themselves. Additionally, they have access to their parents' credit cards and they influence the way their families spend. Experts put the current value of teenagers' spending decisions between two- and three-hundred-billion dollars a year.[3]

All told, America's kids currently control nearly one trillion dollars in annual sales of goods and services in this country, a fact that hasn't escaped the attention of advertisers and marketers. In television commercials aimed at children alone, the industry spent $550 million in 1995. There's big money for those who can successfully influence and manipulate the way kids use their economic muscles and spend their money.

THEY'RE SHOPPERS

Studies show the average six-year-old goes shopping two to three times a week, visiting at least two kinds of stores, one of which is a grocery store. By age ten, this kid is shopping an average of eleven to twelve times a month, visiting as many as five stores in a single week. That's comparable to the number and variety of shopping trips adults make.

Kids under age fourteen don't go to the store to simply look around. They're there to buy something. If they don't find what they came for, they buy something else. It's not the actual purchase but the act of buying that's important.[4]

Time magazine reported that 88 percent of girls between thirteen and eighteen just "love to shop." And they prove it by making nearly 40 percent more trips to the mall than other shoppers.

Today's teens spend most of their money on themselves, are quite picky, and are very opinionated on what they'll buy. They are brand loyal and more attracted to stores by merchandise than by price. They buy everything imaginable—clothing, fast food, magazines, pagers, computers, electronic equipment, music, and entertainment.

The International Council of Shopping Centers reports that teens spend an average of $38.55 per mall visit—not far behind the consumer average of $59.20 for all shoppers. Teenage girls—using a powerful combination of allowances, part-time jobs, birthday cash, and easy access to parents' credit cards—drop an average of $28.95 per week on apparel and accessories.[5]

Cynthia Cohen, president of Marketplace 2000, a Miami research organization that has pulled together the shopping habits of Generation Y, (that group defined as those born after 1976) reports:

Generation Y buyers are highly optimistic. Raised during the rising of the Dow, they have the great optimism that comes from a rising economy. . . . They have their little noses pressed up against the windows of Barneys and Saks. They can't wait to spend their money when they get into their prime spending years. These are mall rats. Malls are their comfort zone. They feel warm and cozy in the malls.[6]

ADVERTISING

Advertising has become such a part of our culture we are mostly unaware of the ways it influences our desires and the way we spend our money.

Some time ago the *New York Times* reported the average American adult is the target of some thirty-five hundred commercial ads in a single day. How outrageous is that? Sure, we live in a highly commercialized society, but thirty-five hundred ads? In a single day? I'll admit that I doubted it so I conducted my own test.

I decided to count the ads I heard or saw over a twenty-four-hour period. I was quite sure I couldn't come anywhere close to the thirty-five-hundred mark.

The next morning the radio alarm sounded and before I could even open my eyes the count was two. So prolific were the ads that morning I could barely keep an accurate count and get ready at the same time.

Of course, I had to count every message, banner, business placard, real estate sign, billboard, license plate frame, bumper sticker, commercial vehicle, and bus I saw on the way to work, all the while being careful not to miss any radio ads. Good thing I wasn't driving.

Reading the newspaper boosted my count significantly even before I made it to the comics. I flipped through a few magazines amazed by how many ads could fit into such a small area. That little known fact sent my count reeling. Logging onto the Internet shot the total through the roof. Then the mail arrived. That's when I surrendered. It was impossible to get anything done while paying such careful attention to counting the commercial influences on my fairly low-key, ho-hum kind of a day. It was mind-boggling. Thirty-five hundred ads per adult per day? I'm a believer.

Back to the kids. How many ads would you imagine invade their little lives? Statistics say that by age seven, children will see some 20,000 thirty-second television commercials a year, 360,000 by the time they reach age twenty (and a full 2,000,000 by age sixty-five, just in case you are curious). And that only accounts for television. Just imagine how many other forms of advertising kids see and hear.

Advertisements, "hidden persuaders," have a subtle yet profound influence on the way we think, act, and respond. The goal is to influence us to believe in and then buy specific brands of goods and services. The younger the target, the easier the task.

When asked why the network spent $30 million to create preschool programs, Geraldine Laybourne, president of Nickelodeon children's television network said, "We recognize that if we start getting kids to watch us at this age, we have them for life. That's exactly the reason we're doing it."[7] Bingo.

The combined forces of manufacturers and retailers, both using a variety of advertising media, have tremendous influence over children. In addition to the direct influence advertising has on children, there's a secondary and even more important effect on the parents. If advertisers want to hook a parent, doing that through the child can be very effective.

Babies are exposed to loads of advertising before they can talk, and it's a given in the industry that toddlers recognize company names before their own. Just imagine how important that fact is to, say, the McDonald's corporation. The kind of marketing required to turn a commercial symbol like the golden arches into a national icon, recognizable by every age group, is the result of brilliant marketing. It doesn't just happen.

Print advertising specifically targeted to kids has skyrocketed in the past few years. Between 1989 and 1993 the number of children's national publications nearly doubled from 85 to 160 without any significant drain from existing magazines. Because of its success and monetary return, advertising aimed at kids through print media will explode in the future.

Because children have such an affinity with computers and things electronic, many marketers are supplementing their outreach to kids by electronic media. To see first-hand the kind of advertising they're using, check out the growing number of kids' sites being established by on-line services. Dozens of marketers like McDonald's, Nike, and Coca-Cola have kid-oriented content on the Internet. Child development experts have identified the five key motivators that influence kids: power, freedom, fun, belonging, and mastery. Effective influence-peddlers strive to make sure kids experience one or more of these emotions while under the influence of their ads. That element becomes more important in making a sale than the product itself.

There's no way to fully describe or measure the influence being brought to bear on the kids of this country. It's everywhere. The messages vary greatly, but the underlying theme is always there nagging, compelling them to buy, and assuring them—*you deserve to have what you want when you want it.*

TELEVISION

Television is the number one marketing tool professionals use to reach kids. Nielsen Media Research[8] reports that kids ages two through eleven watch 21.7 hours of television each week on average. Included in that group are the heaviest viewers—preschoolers—who watch twenty-six hours a week. Granted, this number becomes somewhat skewed by the fact that much of television time for children involves watching a videocassette rather than commercial programming. Still, much of television advertising targets very young children.

According to TV-Free America, a non-profit consumer organization:

The cumulative effect of initiating our children into a consumerist ethos at an ever earlier age may be profound. As kids drink in the world around them, many of their cultural encounters—especially on TV—have become little more than sales pitches, devoid of any moral beyond a plea for a purchase. Instead of transmitting a sense of who we are and what we hold important, today's marketing-driven culture is instilling in [children] the sense that little exists without a sales pitch attached and that self-worth is something you buy at a shopping mall. "No one ad is bad," says Mary Pipher, clinical psychologist and family life author. "But the combination of four hundred ads a day creates in children a combination of narcissism, entitlement, and dissatisfaction."[9]

Teens watch far less television than their younger siblings. Younger teens ages twelve and thirteen watch about twenty hours of television while older teens watch only eight to ten hours a week, a fact that becomes of great concern to advertisers who desperately seek to influence this hard-to-reach but potentially lucrative group.

CHANNEL ONE

Channel One is a television news program targeted at teenagers and beamed to school classrooms around the country by satellite. The programming is offered to school systems at no cost. The company also donates to the schools all the equipment necessary to receive the program (one satellite dish and two VCRs and TVs per classroom). In return the school system must require students to view the program every day.

The twelve-minute daily program consists of ten minutes of news and two minutes of commercials. The program reaches eight million students or 40 percent of all twelve- to seventeen-year-olds in the country.[10]

On the surface the Channel One phenomenon appears to be harmless, perhaps even beneficial. After all, one might argue, teens need to know what's going on in the world. Channel One is the way to get it to them in a format they can understand and will accept—and at no cost to the schools.

Channel One consists of high-tech, fast-paced productions that highlight the commercials rather than the news stories. Their sales literature reads, "Every school day, as many teens watch Channel One as the Super Bowl. Channel One's audience exceeds the combined number of teens watching anything on television during Primetime! Every school day is a Super Bowl! Huge rates. Unsurpassed reach. Unparalleled impact among teen viewers."[11]

Channel One promises to deliver to its big-name corporate advertisers the very hardest-to-reach teen viewers. By terms of the contractual agreements between Channel One and the schools, students must watch the full twelve minutes each day. That means the watching of commercials by this so-called difficult-to-reach teenage audience is mandatory. For this, advertisers like Nike and Pepsi are willing to pay rates that rival those of the Super Bowl—up to two hundred thousand dollars for each thirty-second commercial. That alone is a clear indicator of just how commercially successful Channel One is.

To illustrate that success, consider the Skittles story. Channel One consists of news stories and commercials, however, it is often difficult to distinguish between the two. Producers purposely blur the line between commercials and the news.

A Channel One series of ads for Skittles candy began with what appeared to be a newscaster introducing another news segment. He begins the story when a snowstorm of static suddenly interrupts. As Monty Python-esque images fill the screen, a voice-over says, "We interrupt this class for a temporary fun emergency—for the next thirty seconds think only fun thoughts." A succession of "fun thoughts" follows.

A series of five "fun emergencies" was so successful in boosting sales of Skittles, the company booked ten more spots of the same format for the following season.

Clearly, Channel One has found "success" in influencing and manipulating the buying habits of a huge segment of this nation's teens, those hard-to-reach "light" television viewers. In a society where television ratings are life or death, Channel One doesn't have to worry. Their audiences can't take a bathroom break or click through the commercials. Channel One can count on a captive audience five days a week, month after month after month.

How serious is this influence? *Educational Leadership* magazine reported the findings of a survey of regular

Channel One viewers in their January 1994 issue and concluded, "We found a very strong statistical difference suggesting that regular watching of Channel One reinforces materialistic attitudes."[12]

Just what we didn't want to hear.

THEY ARE UNINFORMED

If I've learned anything from the stacks of mail I've received over the years, it's this: America's kids—churched and unchurched alike—are leaving home without knowing about money, credit, and debt. They're not learning it at school or at home.

At best the subject gets the hit-and-miss approach. In 1996 when *Zillions Magazine* (geared to kids eight years old and up) asked readers how much time they spent during the preceding year learning about managing money, more than 66 percent responded "none."

A national survey of 689 twelve-year-olds conducted by *Consumer Reports*[13] revealed an alarming deficit of basic financial knowledge. For instance: 40 percent of those surveyed didn't know that banks charge interest on loans; 28 percent didn't know that using a credit card was a form of borrowing; and 66 percent thought the amount of advertisement indicates the quality.

A nationwide test of the consumer knowledge of high school seniors[14] found them to be virtually unprepared for the many critical purchasing decisions they will need to make after they graduate from high school.

Teens tested were able to answer only 42 percent of the questions correctly. (Just by guessing they could have statistically scored 25 percent correct.)

The same test given to adults produced curious results. The adults scored only sixteen points higher than the students. Employing even the most liberal scoring procedures, the results are indisputable—everyone flunked.

Four-year college students took a similar test in their junior and senior years.[15] While the results were considerably higher than the high schoolers tested, they didn't come close to passing either. The college students scored an average of 51 percent on thirty-eight questions relating to credit (53 percent), checking and savings (53 percent), auto insurance (58 percent), and life insurance (43 percent).

If all of this financial ignorance isn't bad enough, consider this worrisome fact: Students are financially ignorant but don't know it—and worse, don't care. Here's a snippet of results of The 1997 Phoenix Student Fiscal Fitness Survey of twelve hundred students nationwide.

Only 28 percent could precisely define buying on credit.

Only 28 percent could precisely define a mortgage.

Only 25 percent could precisely define a budget.

Only 7 percent could precisely define life insurance.

Only 4 percent could precisely define Social Security.

Only 5 percent could precisely define compound interest.

Only 3 percent could precisely define mutual funds.

Eighty-eight percent of those surveyed said they are either very good or pretty good at managing their money.

Thirty percent said they are not at all interested in financial information or money matters.

Only 13 percent said they are very interested in such topics.[16]

Cause for concern? You'd better believe it. The most striking finding in the test of high schoolers was how little seniors know about the products and services they will buy after graduation—items like credit, checking and savings accounts, and auto insurance.

By the time college students reach their junior year they have already bought banking and insurance products, rented some type of living quarters, accepted credit cards, and purchased items on credit. And they've likely made considerable mistakes in doing so—mistakes that will have an impact on their futures.

America's youngsters are heading for adulthood unequipped to handle the temptation of easy credit. They are prone to excessive consumerism but lack the financial intelligence they will need to effectively use the economic power they have. It is this power and ignorance, combined with material desires, that makes kids easy marks for the world of commercial influence and consumer credit.

Chapter 8
The Trouble with Debt

— $\$$ —

T hough I find the chore distasteful, I must show you the dark side of consumer debt. The world gives this type of credit living a glamorous spin. It says an approved credit application is a badge of honor, tangible evidence that you are worthy to enter a superior level of consumerism.

You know that I am seriously opinionated about consumer debt. My opinions are anything but positive. For that I do not apologize. Furthermore, I intend to do everything I can to convince you that consumer debt is worse than horrible and hazardous to your children's futures.

Debt-proofing kids requires that the parent pass values to the child. You cannot pass on values you do not possess. For your children to be debt-proofed they must believe with all their hearts that consumer debt is wrong and should not enter their lives. But first you must believe. So while I do care about you, I confess my first concern is for your kids.

And now you know—I have a hidden agenda. I'm using you to get to your kids. Clever, huh?

I didn't learn about debt in a university lecture hall. My classroom has been my life and the lives of thousands of people I've met over the past seven years. I *know* consumer debt—which is light years from just knowing *about* it. Because of my intimate relationship with it, I absolutely despise unsecured consumer debt.

Two Kinds of Debt

Like fireworks, debt comes in two varieties—safe and highly explosive.

Secured debt, like the "safe and sane" fireworks we set off on Independence Day, carries a certain amount of risk. However, if you follow the instructions using ordinary precaution, everything will be just fine.

Unsecured debt (also called consumer debt) is like high-risk, explosive fireworks. Under all circumstances it is extremely dangerous. It promises a spectacular experience and delivers an initial burst of glory. But sooner or later those who think they can play without getting burned wake up with nothing to show for the experience except severe injuries and a pile of ashes.

Secured debt

When the lender holds an asset that has a monetary value equal to the amount of the loan, that loan is secure. The asset acts as the lender's guarantee that the borrower will repay the loan.

The asset is called collateral. If the borrower defaults on the loan, the lender takes the collateral as payment for the loan. The collateral is a "safety valve" to protect both the borrower and the lender. Secured debts are safe debts. Real estate and automobiles are the most common forms of collateral.

Secured debts don't carry a high potential of harm because: 1) the borrower goes through a qualifying process; 2) the protective nature of the collateral provides a way of escape; and 3) interest rates are typically lower on secured loans.

While it is always better not to borrow, we live in a time when it would be impossible for most people to buy a home or automobile without a secured loan. There are circumstances under which secured debt is appropriate.

Unsecured debt

An unsecured debt, or consumer debt, is an uncollateralized loan. There is no security. The borrower exchanges a signature and a promise for the lender's dough.

If the borrower defaults for any reason the lender has the right under the law to come after the borrower, his credit report, and anything else he can get his hands on. Unsecured debts are extremely hazardous because: 1) there is no qualifying process to make sure the borrower isn't in over his head; 2) there is no "safety valve" to protect the parties if things don't go as planned; and 3) interest rates on consumer debt are outrageously high.

The most common types of consumer debt are credit card balances, personal loans, installment loans, and other unsecured obligations, such as dental and medical bills.

Debt makes an arrogant presumption on the future. Let's say you have your eye on a new computer, with a total price of fifteen hundred dollars. You are strapped for cash but have your heart set on it and the store will gladly finance the purchase. You "buy" it for fifteen hundred dollars at 18 percent interest with monthly payments equal to 3 percent of the outstanding balance or ten dollars minimum (very generous terms by the way, given current consumer loan standards). It will take twelve years and three months to pay for the computer. Including interest of $1,298, the real cost of the computer is $2,798.

Beyond the store's refund policy, there is no backing out on this debt. It is unsecured. You owe the money plus interest, no matter what. If you get sick and can't work, you still owe the money. If the computer dies; even if it is stolen, you still owe the money.

Who can predict what will happen in your life over the next twelve years and three months? Will the creditor make allowances for things that might knock you out of kilter? Don't count on it. You will still owe the money . . . no matter what. The creditor will show no mercy.

When you bought the computer you paid for it with credit because you were strapped for cash. Why will things be any different next month? How do you know you'll even have a job, let alone an extra forty-five dollars to make that first payment and all the others right through number 147?

Do you see the arrogance involved in this transaction? By agreeing to pay back $2,798, with absolutely no escape valve, you make a statement that you can foresee the future. You promise to pay this debt based upon an assumption that you will have your health and the abilities you take for granted.

And then there's the little matter of obsolescence. The chances of this computer being anything but a dinosaur in twelve years and three months are slim to none. This country is full of people who are paying for things they don't have anymore with money they don't have yet—and no real assurance they'll ever get it.

To legally obligate oneself to unsecured debt is an arrogant presumption on God's mercy. "You should know better than to say, 'Today or tomorrow we will go to the city. . . .' What do you know about tomorrow? How can you be so sure about your life?" (James 4:13).

"Do not boast about tomorrow, for you do not know what a day may bring forth" (Proverbs 27:1, NIV).

Debt enslaves. Even though written thousands of years ago, King Solomon's wise words are as timely as if they were torn from today's headlines: "The poor are ruled by the rich, and those who borrow are slaves of moneylenders" (Proverbs 22:7).

Slavery is a despicable circumstance. Any loss of personal freedom is degrading and depressing. When you take on unsecured debt, that's exactly what you choose—a form of slavery. Your creditors "own" you as long as you owe them money. Their grip is unrelenting. They are legally entitled to their portion of your paycheck, and you dare not forget that. There are stiff punishments for "slaves" who don't perform for their masters as promised. As distasteful as that thought is, it's an amazingly accurate illustration.

The most curious thing about the slave-master relationship is how some debtors, miserable as they are, keep adding to their debt-load, extending the sentence of servitude with every new purchase.

Debt advances dissatisfaction. Consumer credit enables impulsive spending. Shopping with plastic, the cardholder can make impulsive decisions and purchases. Consumer credit enables instant gratification. When things come too easily, we don't appreciate them. We make silly decisions, impulsive purchases that quickly lose their appeal, leaving us completely unsatisfied with a house full of stuff, a pile of debt, and a raging case of Affluenza. The things we thought would satisfy chokes the joy right out of our lives.

Debt destroys options. When burdened with debt you give up the option to quit a job to return to school, or leave a miserable job to take one that pays less but would allow you to do something you truly love. Debt prevents us from following our dreams or our heart's desire to serve God in some profound way.

I'm reminded of the young woman who knew God was calling her to teach in a missionary school abroad. Her debts, however, were so large she could not quit her present job. She had no resources from which to pay the debts, and so she had to turn down the opportunity to go where she believed God was calling.

Each time you increase your debt you eliminate another option.

Debt destroys relationships. A young man wrote to me recently. It seems the love of his life broke off their engagement because she couldn't see herself starting out married life twenty-three thousand dollars in the hole due to his reckless spending. There was little I could do but encourage him to get busy digging out of the hole so debt doesn't become a pattern of his life. I also told him she did him a big favor. That kind of wake-up call early in life was a gift for which he should send her a thank-you note.

Hideous debt blows up marriages. Debt takes a terrible toll on families, too, not just the spouses.

Debt extends equal opportunity. Never before in the history of this country has credit been so available and debt so attractive. A bank credit card is available to most anyone who has two things: an ID and a pulse. The average non-thinking person views an approved credit application as a badge of honor, a sign he has arrived, the concrete proof he is certainly able to handle this amount of debt. Nothing could be farther from the truth. The credit card issuer sees you as a risk worth taking to increase their profit margins. They don't care if you are income-challenged or have other pressing obligations. It's not their concern if you get in over your head. They're banking on the fact that you'll accept a substantial amount of debt, habitually pay only the minimum monthly payment and never be able to pay the balance in full. Fitting into that profile and operating according to their highest expectations makes you nothing more than a pawn on their chessboard of high finance. Debt does not discriminate. It offers an equal opportunity misery to all.

Debt is hazardous to your wealth. Remember that computer deal we dissected a few pages back? You know, the $1,500 computer that ends up costing $2,798 after twelve years, but has a functional life of only five? With interest the price is almost double the actual price tag.

Now apply that principle to everything bought on credit. People with huge consumer debt have to make twice as much to live half as well as families or individuals who live debt-free. Because their debt obligations are so steep they don't give or save for the future. Debt is a terrible thief.

Debt says we can do this ourselves. God promises to supply our needs. "And my God will meet all your needs according to his glorious riches in Christ Jesus!" (Phillipians 4:19, NIV). I believe it gives God great pleasure to prove his promises in our lives. But when we jump in with our credit cards before we give God a chance to show us his plan, there's an element of "leave me alone . . . I can do this myself, thank you very much!"

By relying so heavily on consumer credit for so many years of my life, I know I shut out God's mercy. I didn't care that his plan might be superior to the one I chose. I thought enough money (or credit) could fix anything.

I'll never know how God planned to take care of us during that time, but I certainly have the scars to prove my way wasn't best. I've learned difficult lessons, ones I hope you and your children will never have to learn as I did. I praise God for his patience, forgiveness, and loving kindness.

Chapter 9
Parenting: It's About Passing On Values

— $\$$ —

P arenting is a curious profession. One of the most challenging jobs in all the universe, it requires no license or degree—not even an entrance exam. And just when you get good at it, your job leaves home without you.

I have been a parent almost as long as I wasn't one, a small piece of trivia that recently piqued my curiosity and sent me in search of a calculator.

The typical worker in this country puts in forty hours a week, fifty weeks a year, for a total of two thousand hours annually.

As a mom I've clocked 168 hours a week, 52 weeks a year (motherhood knows no vacation), or 8,736 hours a year. I have completed 24.5 years or 214,032 hours on the job. Now, by applying the 2,000-hour-work-year standard, I have logged the equivalent of 107 work years as a parent—another interesting but fairly useless piece of information.

My time on the job, and a couple of terrific kids who are still in process (when are kids considered "done," anyway?), may not qualify me as an expert, but it has given me a wonderful opportunity to discover some effective and dependable principles that work to equip kids with the values and financial skills they will need in the real world.

THE MOST CRITICAL PART

It's easy to get so hung up on the mundane side of parenting—cooking, cleaning, carpooling, taxi driving—that we forget about the single most important job parents have to do: successfully pass on our values to our children.

Equipping children with values is not the same as making them obey. Parents can get a kid—even the dog—to do just about anything, provided they exert enough external pressure and a threat of negative consequence. Threats of severe consequences motivate immediate compliance but aren't likely to produce long-term commitment. When the child or teenager is free of the external pressure, his behavior reflects his true values—the condition of his heart—as inappropriate, lacking, or evil as they may be.

Kids who leave home having never taken ownership of positive values, such as integrity, responsibility, courage, and respect, don't make the transition into the real world very well. They bounce around and make all kinds of foolish choices. Often they suffer long-term consequences simply because they do not have a positive, strong value system. They have nothing to guide their lives.

Nothing, not even debt-proofing, is as important in the lives of your children as developing their spiritual sensitivity and then introducing them to the God of the universe who loves them and provided a means by which they can have the gift of eternal life.

Passing to your children the values and financial skills they will need to prosper in the real world is the very heart and soul of debt-proofing—values having to do with the right way to manage money and how to live without debt.

One of the most exciting and gratifying aspects of parenthood is to watch as children assimilate positive values having to do with money, credit, and debt. Even at relatively young ages they will begin to accept responsibility for their choices and behavior. They choose to do the right thing simply because it is right, not to escape external pressure or to earn a reward.

INNER CHOICE

An experiment by psychologist Jonathan Freedman (1965) offers interesting data on this matter of inner choice and accepting responsibility.

> Freedman wanted to see if he could prevent second- to fourth-grade boys from playing with a fascinating toy, just because he had said that it was wrong to do so some six weeks earlier. Anyone familiar with seven- to nine-year-old boys must realize the enormity of the task, but Freedman had a plan.

If he could first get the boys to convince themselves that it was wrong to play with the forbidden toy, perhaps that belief would keep them from playing with it thereafter. The difficulty was making the boys believe that it was wrong to amuse themselves with the toy—an extremely expensive, battery-controlled robot.

Freedman knew it would be easy enough to have a boy obey temporarily. All he had to do was threaten the boy with severe consequences should he be caught playing with the toy. As long as he was nearby to deal out stiff punishment, Freedman figured that few boys would risk operating the robot. He was right.

After showing one boy an array of five toys and warning him, "It is wrong to play with the robot. If you play with the robot, I'll be very angry and will have to do something about it," Freedman left the room for a few minutes. During that time the boy was observed secretly through a one-way mirror. Freedman tried this threat procedure on twenty-two different boys and twenty-one of them never touched the robot while he was gone.

So a strong threat was successful while the boys thought they might be caught and punished. Of course, Freedman had already guessed that. He was really interested in the effectiveness of the threat in guiding the boys' behavior later on when he was no longer around. To find out what would happen then, he sent a young woman back to the boys' school about six weeks after he had been there. She took the boys out of the class one at a time to participate in an experiment. Without ever mentioning any connection with Freedman, she escorted each child back to the room containing the five toys and gave him a drawing test. While she was scoring the test, she told the boy that he was free to play with any toy in the room. Of course, almost all of the boys played with a toy. The interesting result was that of the boys who played with a toy, 77 percent chose to play with the robot that had been forbidden to them earlier. Freedman's severe threat, which had been so successful six weeks before, was almost totally unsuccessful when he was no longer able to back it up with punishment.

However, Freedman wasn't finished yet. He changed his procedure slightly with a second sample of boys. These boys, too, were initially shown the array of five toys by Freedman and warned not to play with the robot while he was briefly out of the room because "it is wrong to play with the robot." This time Freedman provided no strong threat to frighten a boy into obedience. He simply left the room and observed through the one-way mirror to see if his instruction against playing with the forbidden toy was enough. It was. Just as with the other sample only one of the twenty-two boys touched the robot during the short time Freedman was gone.

The real difference between the two samples of boys came six weeks later when they had a chance to play with the toys while Freedman was no longer around. An astonishing thing happened with the boys who earlier had been given no strong threat against playing with the robot: When given the freedom to play with any toy they wished, most avoided the robot, even though it was by far the most attractive of the five toys available (the others were a cheap plastic submarine, a child's baseball glove without a ball, an unloaded toy rifle, and a toy tractor). When these boys played with one of the five toys, only 33 percent chose the robot.

Something dramatic had happened to both groups of boys. For the first group it was the severe threat they heard from Freedman to back up his statement that playing with the robot was "wrong." It had been quite effective while Freedman could catch them violating his rule. Later, though when he was no longer present to observe the boys' behavior, his threat was impotent and his rule was, consequently, ignored. It seems clear that the threat had not taught the boys that operating the robot was wrong, only that it was unwise to do so when the possibility of punishment existed.

For the other boys, the dramatic event had come from inside, not outside. Freedman had instructed them, too, that playing with the robot was wrong, but he had added no threat of punishment should they disobey him. There were two important results. First, Freedman's instruction alone was enough to prevent the boys from operating the robot while he was briefly out the room. Second, the boys took personal responsibility for their choices to stay away from the robot during that time. They decided that they hadn't played with it because *they* didn't want to. After all, there were no strong punishments associated with the toy to explain their behavior otherwise. Thus, weeks later, when Freedman was nowhere around, they still ignored the robot because they had been changed inside to believe that they did not want to play with it.

Adults facing the child-rearing experience can take a cue from the Freedman study. Suppose a couple wants to impress upon their daughter that lying is wrong. A strong, clear threat ("It's bad to lie, Honey, so if I catch you at it I'll cut your tongue out") might well be effective when the parents are present or when the girl thinks she can be discovered. However, it will not achieve the larger goal of convincing her that she does not want to lie because she thinks it's wrong. To do that, a much subtler approach is required. A reason must be given that is just strong enough to get her to be truthful most of the time but is not so strong that she sees it as the obvious reason for her truthfulness. It's a tricky business because this barely sufficient reason changes from child to child. For one child, a simple appeal may be enough ("It's bad to lie, Honey, so I hope you won't do it"); for another it may be necessary to add a somewhat stronger reason (". . . because if you do I'll be disappointed in you."); and for a third child a mild form of warning may be required as well (". . . and I'll probably have to do something I don't want to do."). Wise parents will know which kind of reason will work on their own children. The important thing is to use a reason that will initially produce the desired behavior and will, at the same time, allow a child to take personal responsibility for that behavior. Thus, the less detectable outside pressure such a reason contains, the better. Selecting just the right reason is not an easy task for parents but the effort should pay off. It is likely to mean the difference between short-lived compliance and long term commitment.

As Samuel Butler wrote more than three hundred years ago, "He who agrees against his will is of the same opinion still."[1]

BASIC MONEY VALUES

Values are specific types of beliefs that are so important and central to one's life that they act as life guides. Values are central to a person's personality and responsible for motivations and important decisions that have far-reaching implications. Behavior is the outward expression of one's values.

Debt-proofed kids are guided by a set of values having to do with money, credit, and debt. The parents of debt-proofed kids should be guided by these values too.

I've discovered that most adults don't have a specific value system when it comes to money management, so debt-proofing your kids may well have an added bonus for you. But don't panic. This is easy—so easy you'll wonder why you haven't figured this out sooner.

Here are four simple, but extremely powerful, basic financial values that are part of our family's value system. They are the values we passed on to our children through this process I call debt-proofing. They are so simple even a child can learn and understand, but so powerful accepting them as life guides can turn even the most difficult financial situations around.

Giving

The first part of everything that comes into my life is mine to give back. I give because I am thankful. Giving proves the condition of my heart. It's a thank-you note to God for everything He has given me. It is wrong for me to keep the money that belongs to God.

Saving

I always save part of my money and earn interest on it. It is wrong to spend all of my money and not save some to grow for the future.

Spending

I do not spend more money than I have. I decide if something is a want or need. If I spend all of my money today, I won't have any for tomorrow. I shop wisely. I only buy what I planned, not what's on the display.

Borrowing

I always avoid borrowing money. If I cannot avoid it, I only borrow for things that gain in value and only when I give collateral. I repay my secured debts as quickly as possible. It's wrong to carry unsecured debt.

THE PARENT-CHILD CONNECTION

Do you ever feel like what you say to your kids just bounces off their foreheads? That what you tell them just isn't getting through? That happens to all of us from time to time, but some parents never manage to get through to their kids because they've never truly connected with their children's hearts. They just keep piling on external pressure. Then the kids leave home and completely abandon everything their parents "taught" them. Children throw off external parental pressures the minute they escape the strong arm of authority. If all those lessons and lectures haven't penetrated their hearts and become part of their value system, they'll leave home without them.

Parents need to establish a strong and dependable connection with their kids' hearts. I like to think of it as a channel for communication, the channel through which to deliver life-guiding values.

The way to build this all-important channel is to *know your child*. Sounds pretty mindless, I know. But stick with me—it will make sense.

KNOWING YOUR CHILD IS PRIMARY

It is possible to live under the same roof with people who eat your food and have the same name without ever really knowing them. It happens all the time.

Parents give birth, have this preconceived blueprint of their dream child, and get so busy raising Wonder Child, according to their design and to fit their dreams, they never really know who this person is.

Many homes are filled with cookie-cutter kids. There are lots of these little people who are treated exactly the same way. They receive the same training and the same discipline and they're expected to turn out the same way: perfect.

Charles Swindoll in his book *You and Your Child* says, "You cannot discipline a child you do not love. You cannot love a child you do not know. You cannot know a child if you are not sensitive."[2] Wow! Read that through a few times and let it soak in.

UNIQUE CREATIONS

Every child is a unique creation of God, whole and complete at the moment of birth. This child is unlike anyone in your family or anywhere on earth. Everything he or she is or can become is all there, wrapped up in that tiny bundle.

To realize that God loves us and our children so uniquely that he specifically created each of us with individual characteristics, abilities, and talents is not just awesome—it takes a lot of the pressure off parents to come up with a superior design. God has already taken care of that!

You are the one who put me together
	inside my mother's body,
and I praise you
	because of the wonderful way you created me.
Everything you do is marvelous!
	Of this I have no doubt.

Nothing about me is hidden from you!
I was secretly woven together
    deep in the earth below,
but with your own eyes
    you saw my body being formed.
Even before I was born, you had written in your book
    everything I would do.

                  Psalm 139:13-16

MY LIFE AS A PIANO TEACHER

I taught piano lessons to children of all ages for about ten years. With a top enrollment of about seventy students, I had many opportunities to observe all kinds of parents. I had dominant parents, permissive parents, neglective parents, and, thankfully, many loving-yet-firm parents.

Dominant parents were my least favorite. They were rigid and controlling. Because they decided their child was to become a concert pianist, it was my job to make it happen. They didn't care that there might be other considerations. Like talent. They believed that enough discipline, will-power and determination could change a baseball player into a Beethoven or a bookworm into a Bach.

I could tell within a few sessions if a child had any natural ability. Those students who had talent always did well. They loved to practice and were eager to learn. I couldn't wait for their lessons to hear the progress.

Then there were my talentless kids who showed up each week only because their parents yanked them from their sports or computers to take these stupid piano lessons. They were as miserable being taught as I was teaching them. Who wants to be crammed into a mold that doesn't fit? Who likes to participate through force in something that offers little hope of success? I couldn't help but observe the interaction between these children and their parents. The child's spirit was closed tighter than tight while the angry parents tried to pry their way in. I don't like to think about it, but there is the possibility that something as minor and inconsequential as piano lessons built walls of resentment that have yet to be town down.

Author Gary Smalley in his book *The Key to Your Child's Heart*[3] explains that the dominant parent has very high standards and expectations for the child. This type of parent tends to be unbending and demands strict adherence to a list of rules.

According to Smalley, rigid dominance breaks the spirit of the child and results in resistance, "clamming up," or rebellion. In the end the child usually rejects his parents' rules and their values.

TRAIN 'EM UP

There's a verse in the Book of Proverbs that carries some powerful parenting wisdom.

"Train up a child in the way he should go,
and when he is old, he will not depart from it."

Proverbs 22:6 (KJV)

At first read, you might think this scripture blows holes in my belief that it takes natural talent to become a skilled pianist, that a parent should be able to determine the way a child should go.

Read it again.

In his book *You and Your Child,* Charles Swindoll suggests we can better understand the intent of King Solomon's incredible wisdom if we read it like this: "Adapt the training of your child so that it is in keeping with his God-given characteristics and tendencies; when he comes to maturity he will not depart from the training he has received."[4]

Your primary job as a parent is to know your child. The only way to do that is to devote yourself to the study of your child's natural-born characteristics, tendencies, and abilities. It will be the most enjoyable research you've ever done. The effectiveness of debt-proofing your child will be in direct proportion to the extent you know your child.

THINK GARDENING

I think parents should take lessons from people who love to garden. Gardeners are kind and gentle, patient and nurturing. No matter how dirty they get, they just keep cultivating and encouraging. Only a completely ignorant gardener would ever take a rose bush and attempt to turn it into a pine tree.

Imagine a gardener gets a seed. That's it. Just a tiny, helpless, needy seed. All he knows is that it's one-of-a-kind and more precious than gold. Should he give it full sun or partial shade? Keep it moist or allow it to dry out between waterings? What type of fertilizer? Pest control? Without an instruction manual the gardener won't have those answers until he gets to know this unique gift.

First, he allows the seed to sprout—not out in the cold, harsh world, but in the warmth and shelter of his care. With each day he gains more insight into what he has until he determines the characteristics of this tiny seedling. He studies what great gardeners before him have written about this particular type of seedling. He seeks advice from experts. He is driven to discover the exact conditions it needs for optimum development.

As the seedling gets stronger, he begins to expose it to a variety of conditions that will encourage and develop its natural strengths.

The gardener tends to it every day. He doesn't let it grow wild, but instead supports and trains it to grow into the shape that most becomes its natural characteristics. He feeds it with just the right combination of nutrients and fertilizer. He talks to it and encourages every tiny new shoot. This treasure is his pride, his joy, not because he created it, but because it was a gift that he cared for and nurtured to its full beauty and potential.

Values Are More Often Caught than Taught

This process of knowing your children and adapting their training to fit—not conflict with—their individual "bents," characteristics, abilities, and tendencies is what creates that conduit through which to pass your values.

But exactly how do you make the pass? Through your life. The way you live. Kids learn most effectively through observation and imitation. It's the witness of our lives, more than anything we say, that is taken in slowly and cumulatively by our children.

Children drink in everything around them. They see the way we act with others. They listen to everything we say. They observe the way we handle our money. They hear what we say on the telephone and the way we deal with salespeople. Children compare what they see with what they are told, and in the case of a clear conflict, they usually go with what they see.

Many Ways to Communicate

There are many ways to communicate your values to your kids. There are formal lectures, specific talks, books and discussions of what has been read, reprimands, reminders, various kinds of discipline, punishment, and churchgoing with all of its related activities.

All of these ways of communicating with your kids do count for a great deal, but they cannot come close to the value of your children observing their parents living out their values consistently, specifically, and diligently day in and day out. That's the most sure way to pass on to your kids the values and principles they need to guide their lives—values that will take root in their hearts, not simply stick on the outside until they can get away from your authority.

THIS IS NOT NEW

The importance of passing godly values and important information to the next generation is not a new concept. It was almost time for the people of Israel to cross the Jordan River and conquer Canaan, but God refused to let Moses lead them into the land. Instead, Moses had been told that he was going to die on the eastern side of the Jordan. So Moses gave several farewell speeches to the people of Israel in which he repeated many of God's laws.

Moses also reminded the Israelites about the past forty years. God had rescued them from Egypt and taken care of them in the desert, but they hadn't always been faithful or obedient to him.

Moses told the Israelites that if they kept their agreement to worship and obey the Lord, they would be a successful and powerful nation. But if they broke their agreement and worshiped idols, the Lord promised to put terrible curses on the people. They would be defeated by their enemies and lose their land and their lives.

You can tell just how important it was that they pass the laws to the coming generations by the way their leader Moses instructed them to do it:

"Memorize these laws and think about them. Write down copies and tie them to your wrists and your foreheads to help you obey them. Teach them to your children. Talk about them all the time—whether you're at home or walking along the road or going to bed at night, or getting up in the morning. Write them on the door frames of your homes and on your town gates" (Deuteronomy 11:18–20).

Read that account again, but this time think about your kids and this matter of passing to them financial values— debt-proofing.

First, memorize the four money-related values on page 108. Make copies of them (you can skip the wrist and fore-head action). At the appropriate time, teach them to your children. Talk about them all the time as the subject fits naturally in your family life—when you're at home or walk-ing in the park, when you tuck the kids into bed, and when they get up in the morning.

But most importantly of all, let your kids catch you in the act of living these values!

Chapter 10

Tear Down Attitudes of Entitlement

— $$$ —

For debt-proofing purposes, "entitlement" is that demanding attitude that says "I deserve it even if I haven't earned it or cannot pay for it." Some call it the Gimmes, others the I-Wants. No matter what you call it, this attitude is running rampant, and not only among kids. It affects kids and adults alike.

Entitlement is subtle. It creeps into our lives when we compare our lifestyles and possessions to those of the people we respect and want to be like. It shows up in new parents who throw all caution to the wind when it comes to nursery furnishings and "mandatory" equipment. It shows up in two-income families who, because they work so hard, feel they deserve to have nice things.

Attitudes of entitlement are not limited only to children with desires to have everything they see. It shows up in adults who feel compelled to conform with society's relent- less ratcheting up of standards.

The eighteenth century French philosopher, Denis Diderot wrote an essay entitled *"Regrets on Parting with My Old Dressing Gown."* It seems someone gave Diderot an exquisite gift—a scarlet dressing gown. (Not something your typical guy would get too excited about, but remember this was in the 1700s.) Diderot was so happy to get a new dressing gown he promptly threw his old ratty one away. Curiously, he hadn't noticed how tattered the old gown was because it was comfortable and blended into his surroundings. The contrast between the new scarlet gown and everything else in his study was startling. While he was wearing the gown he couldn't stop noticing the threadbare tapestries, the worn chair, the beat-up bookcases. Piece by piece he replaced everything with something more closely suited to the elegance of his robe. Diderot closes his essay regretting ever receiving the scarlet robe that forced everything else into conformity.

Today, marketing professionals and consumer researchers call this constant reach for conformity the "Diderot effect."

Entitlement is the standard message of marketing and advertising. Look carefully at everything that shows up in your mailbox this week. All the marketing or advertising pieces will carry some underlying message that you deserve this, you need that, you'll never be completely satisfied until you do this or go there. Clothing catalogs point out changes in fashion, linen stores introduce the latest seasonal colors. The message to keep up is relentless. The push for conformity creates attitudes of dissatisfaction and entitlement.

With the explosion in the availability of consumer credit that has encouraged conspicuous consumption, attitudes of entitlement have become all too standard. At every turn it seems something or someone is fanning the flames of entitlement in our and our children's lives.

Attitudes of entitlement, both the parent's and the child's, are an enemy that, if not dealt with, will surely sabotage your efforts to debt-proof your kids.

LIVE AN UNDERSTATED LIFESTYLE

A frugal lifestyle, where you live beneath your means, is the best environment in which to raise kids. When children observe their parents consuming carefully, making wise spending decisions, choosing not to buy the biggest and the best, and not living on credit, they begin to assimilate those values. Rather than always telling your kids, "We can't afford that," a better response is, "We don't choose to spend our money in that way." This sends the message that even though we might be able to afford to buy what you want, too much consumption is not good

Don't aspire to look like the most affluent in the neighborhood by living *as if—as if* you have a big bank balance, *as if* you can afford the cars you drive. If yours is a one-earner family, don't live the lifestyle of your two-paycheck friends. Rather than constantly striving to keep up, look for ways to downshift. Don't live to consume and don't base your self-worth on your net worth.

DISCOVER THE REAL NEED

Attitudes of entitlement are often a symptom. There are times parents get so caught up in the frantic pace of the daily grind they don't realize that most of what children need cannot be bought. Children need time and attention, conversation with their parents, and guidance. They need to know they are significant and valuable and that someone is interested in their moral development. Maybe it's not the new outfit or the CD player that's the real issue after all.

BECOME A GIVING FAMILY

The best antidote for attitudes of entitlement is to give away the very thing you crave. Giving takes our eyes off ourselves and our insatiable desires. It works in children as well. Get your kids involved in supporting your church's outreach ministries. Give to a missionary family that has children of similar ages to yours. "Adopt" an orphan child in a third-world country. There are so many ways your family can become intentional givers. It takes effort and requires commitment, but the benefits both in personal and spiritual growth and in tearing down attitudes of entitlement will be invaluable.

LIMIT SHOPPING

Stay away from malls and throw mail order catalogs in the trash the minute they show up. As much as possible do your necessary shopping solo—without kids. Overexposing children to the grocery store, the mall, or the warehouse club inevitably creates desire. Let the shopping trips that include the children be for a specific purpose, not simply to wander around to see what kind of desire you can create. When the kids are with you in a store make sure you follow the debt-proof rule: Shop with a list, shop with cash, find what you've come to buy, and leave.

LIMIT TELEVISION VIEWING

Monitor children's television viewing. For very young children, select non-commercial viewing. Find a way to let the kids help limit their TV time. Idea: Let the kids decorate popsicle sticks or tongue depressors. Use them to keep track of earned television viewing time. One stick equals thirty minutes of non-family TV time (family viewing is free time for the kids). Devise a plan for the kids to earn sticks (reading books, picking up toys, etc.). Make a rule: no sticks, no TV.

Talk with your kids about commercial advertisements and the real message. Teach them to blow holes in the messages that suggest if you drink a soft drink or buy a certain brand of makeup you'll be like that celebrity. Teach your kids to play the game, "What's the Value?" (could also be called "What's the Lie?"). After each commercial ask them what value the ad was trying to sell. Was it pleasure, possessions, or prestige (prestige could also be power, popularity, or power)? The first person to answer correctly wins.

Commercial advertisements create false need in all of us, but particularly in children. Children are literal in their thinking. Begin looking at this commercialized world through your children's very literal minds. You'll find yourself "believing" all kinds of lies.

If you have children in schools that carry Channel One, rather than forbidding them to participate, prepare them. Have them write down and then report to you the commercials they saw each day along with their assessment of the lie it was trying to tell. Was it pleasure, possessions, or prestige? If you have any influence in the school, suggest that "What's the Value?" might be an excellent follow-up to the daily presentation in class. Everything you do to get your children thinking and making their own evaluations about what the world is trying to make them believe will hasten the day they are debt-proofed.

Consider TV-free periods. Start with a day, go to a full week. It's an enlightening experience.

FIND MALL ALTERNATIVES

Your goal in tearing down attitudes of entitlement is to direct your children's attention and desires away from the commercialization of their lives. Spending less time at the mall and more time in more wholesome venues will support that goal. Create a desire in your children for the library. Capitalize on the fact that most libraries allow us to borrow books, videos, etc., rather than buy them. Push the community aspect of sharing and supporting literature. Attend the special presentations. If your library has a membership fee (many do these days), gladly purchase membership and then use it.

Trade mall time for park time. Make it a point to visit all the parks in your city. Find the hiking trails and bike paths. Call the local Chamber of Commerce to find the factories or manufacturing plants in your area that conduct tours. Make a list of all the places you can be tourists in your own town.

MAINTAIN FINANCIAL PRIVACY

Parents should never tell children how much money they earn. Whether you are at the poverty level or well-heeled, your children should not be privy to your annual income. Kids don't need that information. When they have it they don't know how to interpret it.

One woman shared with me how as a child her entire attitude about life and material things changed the day she learned her father made a six-figure income. Everything shifted as she decided they were the richest people in the world and she deserved whatever she wanted.

If they ask, answer back with the question, "Honey, why do you want to know?" If the child worries you'll be homeless tomorrow, you can respond with comfort of God's care. If your child asks so he can brag to his friends about how rich he is, the answer should be something like, "That is Mommy and Daddy's private information." It is OK for parents to have financial privacy.

DITCH CREDIT, DEBIT, AND ATM CARDS

Credit cards, debit cards, telephone withdrawals, and ATM cards are stand-ins for money—they are not the real thing. They confuse the issue of who's paying for what. It's important that you make money real for your kids and that they observe you living in that reality as well. Parents should live a cash lifestyle before their children. Kids shouldn't see your plastic. They shouldn't see you use it, and they shouldn't see it in your wallet.

Children are very literal. This is what children see when you pay for goods or services with a credit or debit card: Someone "swipes" the card through the machine, the little clicking sounds commence, you sign your name, and then you get the card back, plus the merchandise too. What the child sees is that you got something for nothing because you have a plastic magic key. It doesn't matter to them if you pay the entire bill in full every month or that your debit card is actually taking money directly from the checking account. Kids cannot process abstract thoughts. Even your older children don't need to see you living contrary to the values you are teaching them. Remember, debt-proofed kids live a cash lifestyle. Seeing their parents live that way, too, validates those family values.

What about ATM transactions? Same thing. Kids see you put a piece of plastic in the wall (these days, credit, debit, and ATM cards all look alike) and what happens? Clicking sounds and you get back the card and free money! It didn't cost you anything. All you need is a plastic key.

ATM cards, credit cards, debit cards, and checkbooks should be used, if at all, out of the presence of kids. When kids are around, it's cash only.

HOLIDAYS

There's nothing like the Christmas holidays to encourage entitlement fever in all of us. But there are lots of things you can to do keep this holiday in line with your new understated lifestyle. First, make the season a time of giving and sharing. It's a perfect time of the year to help your kids go through their toys and clothes to scale back and downsize in anticipation of some new stuff. Let the kids go with you to deliver them to a shelter or to a needy organization. At the time of year your time is most valuable, give that precious gift to your kids. Spend time, make memories, have fun. Impose reasonable limits on the length of wish lists. Don't enable longing and yearning by the presence of catalogs and toy store magazines in your home. Help your kids make gifts. Measure carefully every activity so that it fits into a larger picture of making this a time we give more than we receive. Point to the symbolism of giving and the real reason we celebrate.

GRANDPARENTS AND OTHER BENEFACTORS

I'm not a grandmother but hope to be someday. Just between you and me, I'm a little worried because of my natural propensity to overindulge. But I'll say what I need to say and hope I have the presence of mind to remember this when the time comes.

Grandparents often sabotage good work that has gone on between the parents and child by feeling they must always be gifting the grandchild. If you give too much and too often, you interfere with the principles and values the family is establishing.

Bob and Dot, who have several grandchildren and hope to have more, have hit upon what appears to be a great plan. Upon the birth of each grandchild they open a mutual fund custodial account for the baby's education. Then for each grandchild's birthday they give one nice outfit, one special toy, and a deposit into the investment account. At Christmas each grandchild receives one nice outfit, one special toy, and a gift certificate to a profession-al photographer. I love their plan because it's something the parents can plan on (especially those regular trips to the photographer), it's not over-indulgent, and it frees Bob and Dot during the rest of the year to just have fun with their grandchildren without the kids always expecting a gift.

BIRTHDAYS

A child's birthday should be the best day of the whole year. Set a spending limit ahead of time and keep to the cash-only rule. Think of ways to make the child feel special that don't involve gifts and lots of money. Decorate his room with balloons. Make it a no-chores day for the birth-day child. Treat her like a princess for a full twenty-four hours. If you have a traditional party, keep a lid on the quantity of gifts as much a possible. I know of families who designate certain birthdays the big milestones (five, ten, sixteen, eighteen) having parties at those years, and opting for family celebrations in the years between.

But of all the times that you want to convey to your children how wonderful they are, and how thankful you are for them, it's on their birthdays.

By far the best antidote for entitlement attitudes is to put your children into the debt-proof plan of this book. Going "on salary" at about age ten will put the brakes on attitudes of entitlement as your child begins to control his or her own desires and perspectives, from the inside out.

Clearly, attitudes of entitlement are a serious problem. But they are not terminal. Diligent parents who are willing to be consistent examples and limit-setters will find success in tearing down these attitudes that have the potential to do great harm.

Chapter 11

Build Financial Intelligence

— $\$$ —

I t takes relatively little effort to teach kids about money. And the payoff is enormous. If you are diligent to work this teaching into the normal course of family life it will come as naturally as teaching kids good manners or how to do laundry. It will be as ordinary as teaching them how to mow the lawn or wash the car.

Think of this chapter as a menu of basic money facts your children need to know, along with ideas and suggestions for how you can present them in a kid-friendly way. Not a one-time lesson, this information will be best taught—with the intention that it will be caught—as it is lived out in your home.

MONEY MANAGEMENT

At the foundation of your children's financial intelligence should be this undeniable truth: It is not the amount of money you have, but what you do with it that matters. This is true for a child managing a five-dollar-a-week allowance or an corporate executive with a five-thousand dollar-a-week salary.

For many years of my life I didn't know this truth. On the contrary, I believed that more money was the answer. I was convinced that if we just made more money, won the lottery, or received some unexpected inheritance, all of our money problems would vanish. But the more we made the worse our problems became. Because I didn't know how to manage what we had, more would have never been enough. We didn't save, we didn't give, we didn't plan, and we had no idea where all the money went.

Unless your children learn simple, wise money management techniques, more money will never be enough.

Teaching kids money management

Tell stories. A great way to teach this basic of all financial truths is through storytelling. Here's one of my favorites—a true story—that you can tell your kids.

A man who lives in Ohio went to work straight out of high school for minimum wage. He was a common laborer, a blue-collar worker. He didn't make much money, so every time the local electricity company raised their rates, it was a major financial struggle for him and his family. It didn't take long for him to become discouraged; the harder he worked to make a living, the more it seemed his money was being gobbled up by this big, rich utility company.

One day he had an idea about how he could change his attitude toward this greedy company. He would become a part owner in the company, not because he was wealthy but because he was a smart money manager.

His electricity company, like most utility companies, has a program that allows customers to purchase stock in the company. The man decided that each month when he paid his electricity bill he would send a second check equal to one-day's wages to purchase stock in the company.

In some way, sending that second check every month made paying his electric bill easier because he knew he was actually making a payment to his company and at the same time increasing his ownership. The secret is he never missed a month. Over the years whenever he received a raise, he increased his monthly purchase so that it always equaled one-day's wage.

I am told this man is now one of the largest stockholders in that local electricity company—a multi-millionaire—not because he switched to a big paying job but because he learned how to manage the small amount of money he made from his regular, low-paying job. It was all a matter of wise and consistent money management.

Troll for stories. Share with your kids stories you read and hear about people who, like the man from Ohio, illustrate this principle of money management. Negative examples are also effective. Watch for stories of people who win the lottery, live like a king, and in no time at all file for bankruptcy because they just didn't know how to manage money. Stories like that are amazingly common.

The jar system. It's simple, it's cheap, and it works really well. Take empty, clear glass or plastic jars and label them appropriately: "Needs," "Long-term savings," "Short-term savings," "Giving," "Spending" and so on. Even preschoolers understand the jar system. Teach your kids how to split their money according to your family's basic money management rules.

The least kids need to know about money management:

1. It's not how much money you make, but how you manage what you have that matters.

2. You don't need a lot of money to be a good money manager. Even a small amount of money well managed is far more important than a lot of money wasted.

3. In the same way you have life rules by which you live, you need money rules that guide the way you handle your money.

GIVING

I believe that God has designed a perfect plan when it comes to money. It's simple. We are to give back the first part of everything we receive. Giving away part of the money that flows into our lives exposes our lives and our finances to God's supernatural intervention. Giving proves we trust God to take care of us, builds our faith, and acknowledges our dependence on God's mercy. It is an affirmation that every good thing comes from God.

The conduit through which God chooses to deliver the money we need may be a job, an investment, an inheritance, or some other means—but he is the source. The delivery system may change a thousand times during our lives, but God is unchanging. All he asks is that we give back the first part of everything he gives to us.

Teach your kids to always give back to God 10 percent of their income before they save or spend. Teach kids a value: I always give away part of my money.

This giving principle is really simple to teach to young kids. They don't question, they don't try to reason. They will simply believe you when you teach them that spending all of your money is a selfish thing to do. Because kids are anxious to please, they respond very well to the idea that it makes God happy when we are thankful and give him part of everything we get. It is a good habit to become a giver.

Teaching your kids about giving

Reasons to give. Brainstorm with your child good reasons to give. It helps people who are less fortunate or who are sick. It helps missionaries. It helps you focus on the needs of others. Giving money helps you become a responsible person. When people only think of themselves they become selfish and "self-centered." Giving makes the world a nicer place to live. Think about this: If everybody became a giver there would be fewer hungry kids.

Ways to give. Maybe you have seen people put money in the offering at church. That is a good way, because the leaders of the church are wise, and God helps them decide where that money in the offering should go. There are also other places you can give in your community like homeless shelters or rescue missions. Together with your child, make a list of ten organizations to which your child may give money. Help your child learn more about each organization and decide on one or more to which to contribute. Once you think like a giver, you will keep your ears open for special needs.

The least kids need to know about giving:

1. Giving always comes first, before any saving or spending.

2. Giving 10 percent should be a minimum.

3. There are many places and ways to give. You can watch your money help in many different kinds of circumstances.

SAVING

Saving money means choosing to keep it in a safe place instead of spending it. No matter how small the amount of money your kids receive, saving part of it should be a given. Saving money will become a lifelong habit in no time at all if it is approached as mandatory to right living. There are several kinds of savings that your kids need to learn about.

Teaching your kids about saving

Long-terms savings. Think of this as serious savings— money that you don't touch, borrow, or spend. Adults call it retirement savings, kids don't need to call their long-term savings anything specific. It's the act of always saving for the long-term that is important.

Long-term savings should be kept in an interest-bearing account and left to grow. Teaching kids from a young age to always pay themselves first before they spend will help this become a habit when they are grown.

Your child's long-term savings should be kept in a safe interest-bearing account. Some banks and credit unions still offer simple school savings accounts where minimums and fees are waived. Once a significant amount has been saved, consider moving long-term savings into a more aggressive vehicle such as a mutual fund account where the child is the account owner and the parent is the custodian.

Short-term savings. This is the way you teach your kids to accumulate enough money to buy something that costs more than they have on a weekly or monthly basis, such as a bike, new doll, or computer game. Short-term saving teaches the joy of delayed gratification and the value of truly yearning for something. "Save first, spend later" is a motto your kids won't learn at the mall or from television, but a sound principle they need to learn from you.

Because kids are so literal, providing some kind of visual aid will help them see and understand the principle of saving to buy things that cost more than they receive in a week or a month.

Collecting the money in a jar is a good idea. Here's another idea to help visualize the joy of short-term savings.

Find a picture that represents the items he wants. Maybe it's a bike or special toy. Make a chart or poster and attach the picture to the top. Calculate the full price of the item including tax. Divide this by the amount the child elects to put into short-term savings to determine how many saving periods will be required.

Mark off large squares below the picture representing the periods it will take to save the money he'll need. Inside each square write the amount to be saved. Attach an envelope to the poster. Each time your child receives his income, he can place the stipulated savings amount in the envelope and mark off the square. Each time a savings deposit is made into the envelope and a square is marked off, he sees himself moving closer to the goal.

Saving money consistently is like riding a bike or learning to type. At first the activity is awkward and a little shaky. It might not feel right or even fair. But through consistent practice—repeating the same action over and over again—the activity will become automatic.

If you develop in your children the habit to always pay themselves before they spend or pay others, saving will be as much a part of their lives as anything else you teach them to do on a regular basis.

The least kids need to know about saving:

1. If you always save some of your money—before you even think about spending—you will never be broke.

2. Long-term savings (money that you leave alone so it can earn interest over a long period of time) is mandatory. It's just the right way to manage money.

3. Short-term savings (money you accumulate for something you want) is optional.

4. Saving money can be as gratifying as spending money. The difference? The good feeling you get from saving goes on and on while the fun of spending fun doesn't last very long.

NEEDS AND WANTS

Is it a necessity or a luxury? Essential or optional? We live in a culture where the lines between needs and wants have become terribly blurred. I communicate with people all the time who insist that cable television is an essential expense or that not one but two cell phones are an absolute necessity. No wonder kids are so mixed up on this subject of needs and wants.

Spending is probably the first financial concept your kids will understand. Even toddlers have an uncanny ability to make the connection between money and stores. Giving, saving, and investing, however, have to be taught, as does distinguishing between different types of spending. That's where the necessity for teaching the difference between needs and wants comes in.

Needs are necessities, things we must have to live—things like shelter, clothes, food, and medicine. Wants are things that we like that make our lives fun and enjoyable. It is not wrong to want things. Sometimes it is good to want things that make our lives easier or more enjoyable. However kids must learn that needs come first, and even adults cannot have everything they might want.

Teaching your kids the difference between needs and wants

Need vs. Want Game. It takes practice to tell the difference between a need and a want. You can play informal games with your kids during a meal, in the car, or at other times to help them learn. Let television commercials, print ads, or billboards be your game material. Have the kids determine if the product advertised is a need or a want. The first one with the right answer—and explanation—wins that round. You should expect some lively conversations, especially with your older kids or teens. For example, you see an advertisement for Nike tennis shoes. Is that a need or a want? Well, shoes are a need but the Nike brand name is a want—often a very expensive upgrade. That observation could easily lead to a conversation about brand loyalty and why customers feel pressured to spend twice the price just to get a certain brand. Do they think they will be like the celebrity who endorses that brand? Is it emotional appeal? Belief in misleading claims?

What If Game. Have your children answer this question: What if I could have everything I want? First they must make a list of all the things they would have if they could have everything they want. Next they need to answer questions like: Where would I keep everything I want? How would I make sure they were safe and secure? How would I enjoy all of these things? It doesn't take long for a child to understand that having everything we think we want can pretty much ruin our lives.

The least kids need to know about needs and wants:
1. Needs are essential, wants are optional.
2. It is not wrong to want things. Just remember you your wants will always exceed your means.
3. A true need is never realized while you are in a store. If you really needed it, you knew that before you left home.

SPENDING RECORD

A spending record is a tracking device. It shows where the money went. Money has a way of slipping through your fingers just as if you tried to pick up a handful of water.

Teaching your kids to keep a written record of where their money goes (every cent!) is a habit that will impact their futures tremendously. Tracking expenses in a written format demands focus and keeps spending on a more intelligent level. A written spending record has the effect of plugging up money leaks. Start them young and the process will become a lifelong habit.

The purpose in all of this is to teach your kids to balance income and expenses, a skill that will come in handy once they are out on their own.

Teaching your kids about a spending record

While it would not be advisable to expect a spending record from a preschooler, an older child can easily be required to keep a log of where his money goes. Some parents go so far as to "replace" only the amount of money the

child can account for in writing. For example, a child receiving a $50 a month salary would have to produce a spending
record that accounts for all of that amount (including saving
and giving) in order to receive the next month's salary. That
is a severe measure, but could be quite effective.

Teach your children that "to whom much is given,
much is required." When we receive money, we must be
responsible with it. Keeping a record of where our money
goes is the way we become good money managers. A
spending record keeps money from leaking out of our lives.

Get a notebook. Use this notebook as a spending record
for your child. Show your child how to write down all expenditures—i.e. $10 - long-term savings, $10 - church offering,
$2 - short-term savings, $3 - movie ticket, etc. The goal is
that the spending record will balance with his or her income.

After a few months your child will be ready to move on
to the spending plan. All of the data gleaned from the
spending record (where the money went) can be used to
make a written plan of where it will go next month.

The least your kids need to know about a spending record:

1. It is important to keep track of where your money
goes. Write it down.

2. During the month keep comparing your spending
record with your income. It won't take long for you to make
them come out the same. For instance if you get ten dollars
a week as allowance, or salary, your spending record at the
end of the week should add up to ten dollars, because you
will have written down every cent you gave away, saved,
and spent.

3. A spending record is the way to make sure money doesn't leak out of your life without your approval.

Spending Plan

Some people call it a budget. Personally that word give me a rash, so I prefer the term spending plan. Your kids will too!

A written spending plan is simply the easiest way to match income to expenses. A spending plan is like a road map. It shows you where you are, where you need to go and how to get there. Even a young child can learn to write down how she plans to spend her money.

Teaching your kids about a spending plan

To help your child understand the need for a written plan, use the example of building a house. It would be foolish for a contractor to go to the lumberyard, buy a truck load of wood, dump it on an empty lot and just start building. No builder in his right mind would set out to do something important like building a house without a plan. It's called a blueprint.

A spending plan is simply a blueprint that helps you build your financial life. Kids can understand the need for making a plan when something is really important. When you plan ahead of time how you will spend your money, you have control over it. You make the decisions. If you don't make a plan and just spend it for any old thing without much thought, you lose control. It's not critical at first, but if you start a pattern of losing control, after a while your money will control you.

To make a spending plan, gather information from a past spending record or two. Using this information help your child plan how he will spend his money the next month. Decrease spending? Increase short-term savings? Add an additional short-term savings goal?

The least your kids need to know about a spending plan:

1. You should always make a simple written plan for how you intend to spend your money ahead of time. Your spending plan should include your plans for giving and saving.

2. A plan that is not written down is only a dream. You might think you can remember your plan in your head, but it's always better to write it down.

3. You can make a weekly spending plan or a monthly plan—whatever works best for you. Keep it in a special place where you can refer to it often.

4. Every month when you make a new spending plan, adjust it according to what happened last month. Example: If you planned to spend $3 on a ticket to the movies but ended up spending $4.50 because you bought a snack, remember what happened if you plan to go to the movies again. Make that adjustment so your plan and your actual spending match.

BANKING

Teaching your older kids the concept of banking can be done in a variety of ways. If you live close to a bank you can use the real thing by taking the older child in to meet a teller, learning about deposits and endorsing checks. Younger children, however, might respond more favorably to a family banking system as a precursor to the traditional institution.

The Bank of Mom and Dad might work like this: Set up a system complete with checkbooks and deposit slips. Let the kids deposit their allowances with you and write checks against that Bank of M&D when they want to give, save or spend their money. Show kids how to keep a check register (doesn't preclude the need for a spending record) and keep a running balance of what's in their account. The banker's job of course is to either pay the check or bounce it if there are insufficient funds.

One father I heard from set up the Bank of Dad. His very generous interest bearing accounts taught even his five-year-old the joy of watching his money grow. His rule was that money left in the family bank for more than one week began earning interest.

Another family followed the traditional Jamaican custom call su-su. In essence, the family forms a partnership with each member agreeing to deposit a specific amount at a specific time each month. Then, each month the entire bank goes to one member of the family partnership with everyone taking a turn. By the end of a full cycle, each family member has had the joy of receiving one large sum of money. No interest is involved, but this does eliminate the element of risk and teaches kids that consistent saving results in great benefit.

Whatever method you use, it is important that the concept of traditional banking, including checking and savings accounts, be taught to your kids early enough that they feel comfortable with it by the time they leave home.

Teaching your kids about banking

You might have to schedule an intentional trip to the bank to show your kids how it works. Call ahead and get an appointment with a bank official who will show your kids the vault and explain how the operations work.

Older kids and teens should learn the fundamentals of reconciling a checking account. If you are not in the habit of doing this, start. If you have a home computer you might consider simple accounting software that allows you to track and reconcile your checking account electronically. Your kids will pick this up quickly!

Make sure your kids know how to fill out a deposit slip and a check and how to endorse and deposit checks.

The least your kids need to know about banking:

1. There are two kinds of bank accounts: savings accounts that pay you interest and checking accounts that allow you to spend at will.

2. Banks are safe. If you put money in a bank you won't have to worry about losing it because banks and credit unions are federally insured. That means the federal government guarantees that if the bank goes out of the business, the depositors will get their money back, up to $100,000.

3. When you are old enough to have a checking account it is very important that you keep good records. If you write checks for more money than you have, your checks will bounce and you will be heavily fined.

4. While checks are a safe way to send money through the mail, living with cash on a day-to-day basis is a lot simpler because when it's gone, it's gone!

5. It is illegal to write a check for more money than you know you have in the bank.

AUTOMATIC TELLER MACHINES

The use of automatic teller machines (ATMs) is a privilege extended to experienced bank customers. Visiting the ATM on a regular basis can be hazardous to your wealth, because it is so easy to get money from one's account. The best way that an adult can make an ATM both convenient and safe is to visit rarely and track spending impeccably. Taking the time to go into the bank and deal with a real teller (unless of course you bank now charges a fee for such a privilege) takes extra time but does keep us in better contact with the whole concept of deposits and withdrawals.

Teaching your kids about ATMs

Looking at ATMs through a child's eye and mind will help you understand how necessary it is for her to understand how this works. ATMs are not money-making machines. The ATM card is not a magic key. There is a limit to the amount of money a person can withdraw from their account using the ATM.

Teach your kids that convenience often comes at a cost. Using ATM machines frequently can be costly because some of them charge a fee just to use the machine. Share experiences you might have had using an ATM only to be charged a fee to take out your own money!

The least your kids need to know about ATMs:

1. Automatic Teller Machines are for adults. An ATM is like a robot. The bank can hire fewer tellers if they have an ATM to help customers with their money.

2. An adult needs a secret code called a PIN in order to get some of their money out of the ATM.

3. An ATM card is not a credit card. It's more like a "permission card" that allows a bank customer to withdraw some of their money without the need for a teller.

4. It is very important to keep track of all ATM withdrawals just as if you wrote a check or went into the bank and made an in-person withdrawal.

5. Most banks do not charge their own customers to use an ATM. However, using the ATM owned by another bank will cost a fee.

CREDIT CARDS

As a parent you should think of a credit card as a live hand grenade. In your child's possession it could go off when you least expect it and cause some serious damage. A child or teen does not need to have or use a credit card to learn everything there is to know about them. You want to teach your children that a credit card can be either used or abused. When used, it becomes a very helpful tool that makes some things in life more convenient. When abused, credit cards—and the resulting debt—can make life miserable.

Credit card rules are simple: Never use a credit card to pay for something because you do not have enough money. If you use a credit card to secure a rental car or to pay for something you order over the phone or through the mail, always pay the balance in full within the grace period (the period of time when no interest will be due, typically twenty-five days).

An adult needs only one all-purpose credit card.

Teaching your kids about credit cards

Just because kids don't use credit cards or observe their family living on credit doesn't mean they cannot learn all about them.

Use credit card applications that come in the mail to explain interest rates and all of the terms and conditions. Talk about how credit cards have become the tender of choice in most retail establishments. These days only about 30 percent of those purchases made are paid in full during the grace period. The rest become consumer debt because the cardholder pays only a tiny amount every month.

The least kids need to know about credit cards:

1. A credit card purchase creates a loan. You don't really own something bought with a credit card until you pay the bill.

2. Responsible adults use a credit card as a helpful tool and to build a solid credit history, not to buy things because they don't have enough money. That is why they only need one all-purpose credit card.

3. Abusing a credit card means using it to buy more things than you have the money to pay for. Carrying a credit card balance from month to month is very expensive because of the high interest.

4. If you buy something with a credit card and then pay it off in low monthly payments, you will end up paying for it three times! A one-hundred-dollar CD player would cost about three hundred dollars—and it would take many years to pay for it. Chances are the CD player will not last as long as it takes to pay for it.

5. Credit card debt is the biggest reason so many families have to file for bankruptcy in this country.

Debt

There are only two kinds of debt: secured and unsecured. Unsecured debt is the killer because there is no collateral involved. If a person defaults on an unsecured obligation, the creditor comes after the person and his credit report.

Unsecured debt is dangerous because when not paid in full in a very short period of time it accrues huge amounts of interest quickly. Unsecured debt should be avoided at all costs.

Secured debts involved collateral and that is what makes them "safe debts." If you can't make the payments, the lender can take the collateral the debtor has put up to secure the loan in exchange for full payment. Secured debts include house loans and car loans.

Teaching your kids about debt

Make sure you kids know the difference between secured and unsecured debt. If you have debts you regret, tell your kids about it, if you are comfortable. You might want to admit that you've made some mistakes in the past and now you are doing everything you can to pay them off quickly. Kids don't need to know all the details or to carry the burden of anxiety over family finances.

While kids should find borrowing money abhorrent, if it happens that you decide to make them a loan, require collateral. Make sure it is something as valuable as the amount they are borrowing and then take possession of it. The child should not have use of the collateral during the loan period in order to experience the full impact of debt.

Let's say for example your young teen must borrow fifty dollars for some reason and offers his CD player as collateral. Physically remove the item from his room and keep it in yours. Write up a promissory note, along with the condition that if payment is not made as agreed, the CD player becomes yours to sell in order to recover the debt.

Share stories and articles you read that pertain to consumer and other types of debt.

Teach your kids what the Bible says about debt. Relate times that you've felt like a slave because of debts you incurred.

Make a chart of a debt-payment schedule that you feel comfortable sharing with your kids. If you have a mortgage, this might make a good visual. Post the payment schedule on the refrigerator showing how much of the payment each month goes toward interest, and how many more payments will be required to pay it in full. You'll be shocked, as will your kids!

The least kids need to know about debt:

1. Unsecured debt is the dangerous, killer type of debt because if you have trouble making the payments you don't have a remedy.

2. Secured debts are safer debts because the value of the collateral provides security for both the borrower and the lender.

3. Never borrow money for something that will lose its value quickly or be used up in less than three years.

4. It is always best to avoid debt, but if you cannot, in the case of buying a house or a car, make sure the debt is secured and that you pay it off as quickly as possible.

5. Debt-free is a wonderful way to live. You can live on a lot less money if you have no debts and you have a lot more options.

CONSUMERISM

It's a fine line we walk when it comes to teaching our kids to be smart consumers. On the one hand we do not want to glorify shopping and overconsumption, but on the other we need to teach skills such as getting the best value for the best price and knowing how to make a return. A lot of this kind of teaching can happen at home—prior to the shopping trip and away from the influence of the mall environment. The fact that your kids will be spending their own money before they are too old will help them become savvy consumers. Kids are far less anxious to let go of their own money. When they do only to end up with a junky toy or other disappointing purchase, a valuable lesson is in consumerism is learned.

You want to teach your kids how to match quality with need (don't spend a lot for a trendy item that will be here today and gone tomorrow), to keep receipts in case an adjustment needs to be made, to shop for the best value, to anticipate sales and to shop out of season.

Teaching your kids about consumerism

It takes two groups of people to make stores work: manufacturers who make things and consumers who buy what they make. Whenever you spend your money to buy something you become a consumer. Some people become out-of-control consumers because they buy more than they need.

Responsible consumers are careful to find the best value for things they truly need or will use. Otherwise they are simply wasting their money. Let's say you have save enough money to buy a bike.

Responsible consumers comparison shop. They check around in different stores to find the best price for the items they need. You go to three different bike stores and write down the three different prices. You compare features and guarantees. Careful consumers don't make decisions quickly. They take time to think so they make the best choice. Sometimes the cheapest choice is not the best choice. If you are shopping for something that needs to last a short time (like a swimming suit—you're going to grow before next summer) you should probably look for the cheapest price. This is called matching quality with need. On the other hand, if something needs to last a long time (like an appliance), it would be silly to buy the cheapest one if that means it won't be reliable. Paying a little bit more to get something that will last would be a much better choice. A wise consumer does research to find out which products are recommended by experts.

As a consumer you should expect satisfaction. That means if you buy something and it doesn't work or doesn't fit right, you can take it back for an exchange or a refund. Smart consumers are polite and courteous. Always treat store employees the way you would like them to treat you.

Teaching your kids to be responsible consumers

When a child is with you at the supermarket teach him to compare prices. Most stores these days disclose the per-unit price, making it simple for a child to see which box of cereal is the better value.

Help your children check for quality when making a purchase.

Allow kids to observe you handling a customer service situation where you need to return an item or make an exchange. Teach them to save their receipts and to understand store policies about such matters.

Help your children comparison shop once they've saved the money for that new bike or special outfit. Go to several stores and write down prices and features. Spend time comparing. Find out if the item of interest will be going on sale any time soon. Encourage them to sleep on their purchasing decision for at least twenty-four hours. Minds do change!

Teach kids how to match quality with need. A growing girl doesn't need the quality of a hundred-dollar pair of shoes. She won't wear them long enough to warrant the investment. A single grandmother wouldn't need an extra-capacity, heavy-duty washing machine, but a family with twelve kids would.

The least kids need to know about consumerism:

1. Responsible consumers spend their money wisely and make smart choices.

2. Consumers have the right to full satisfaction. If you are not happy with the quality or performance of something you buy, return it for a refund or exchange.

3. The best value may not always be the item with the cheapest price.

4. Buying things second-hand or used is a great way to get what you need at a bargain price.

CREDIT REPORTS

Credit files are just a fact of life in this country. There's no way to avoid it, so the best course of action is to make sure you and your kids have clean, positive credit histories.

A credit report is used for more these days than simply qualifying a person for new debt. Many employers look at a credit report to learn of the job candidate's true character. Late payments and credit charge-offs say a lot about the way a person conducts his or her life.

Insurance companies and landlords typically request a person's credit report before making a decision.

Teaching your kids about credit reports

You can teach kids a lot about life and consequences of behavior with a credit report. Order a copy of your own report (if it does not have information you wish to keep private from you kids—in which case ask the credit bureau to send you a sample report) and go over it with them. It will look like Greek in the beginning, but persistence will pay off. The report will come with instructions on how to read it and how to report any erroneous information.

Your children will need to establish their own credit reports. I suggest by about age twenty. This will automatically open a credit history file in which their credit report will be housed, a report that will stay with them for life.

Teach your children that a credit report is like an report card. Once negative information like late payments on bills are on a credit report, they stay there for many years. It is impossible to have them "fixed" or erased. You can, however, have incorrect information removed, and you should! You wouldn't want someone else's poor character keep you from renting an apartment or getting a job.

The least kids need to know about credit reports:

1. A credit report is a financial report card. It is like a permanent school record. A school record keeps track of a kid's grades, activities, and accomplishments. Every adult has a credit record that is kept by a company called a credit bureau or a credit reporting agency.

2. When you apply for a credit card, a credit report is opened in your name and kept in the files of the credit bureaus.

3. No one can look at your credit report without your written permission. When you apply for a job or an apartment the company owner or landlord may ask your permission to see your credit report.

4. Because a credit report shows how you are with paying your bills and keeping your word, it becomes more of a character report.

5. Once a year go over your credit report (order it from the bureau) to make sure all of the information is correct. It will come with instructions on how to make corrections to erroneous information.

COMPOUND INTEREST

Teaching kids about compound interest gives meaning to act of saving and investing money. That's what makes it fun. Compound interest is remarkable, as demonstrated by the schedule below. Michael and Justin both decided to save one thousand dollars a year. The problem is, Michael started right away and then stopped after eight years, leaving the money in an investment earning 10 percent compounded annually. While it is not recommended that anyone set out to be as foolish as Michael and stop saving after only eight years, even that is much more intelligent than starting later, as did Justin. Even with the consistency of Justin's savings program once he got over his procrastination, he was unable to catch the growth of Michael's account. That's because of the phenomenon of compound interest. The moral of the story is this: Sooner is better than later.

AGE	Michael Invests	Total after Compounding Interest	Justin Invests	Total after Compounding Interest
22	$ 1,000	$ 1,100	0	0
23	$ 1,000	$ 2,310	0	0
24	$ 1,000	$ 3,641	0	0
25	$ 1,000	$ 5,105	0	0
26	$ 1,000	$ 6,716	0	0
27	$ 1,000	$ 8,488	0	0
28	$ 1,000	$10,437	0	0
29	$ 1,000	$12,581	0	0
30	0	$ 13,839	$ 1,000	$ 1,100
31	0	$ 15,223	$ 1,000	$ 2,310
32	0	$ 16,745	$ 1,000	$ 3,641
33	0	$ 18,420	$ 1,000	$ 5,105

34	0	$ 20,262	$ 1,000	$ 6,716
35	0	$ 22,288	$ 1,000	$ 8,488
36	0	$ 24,517	$ 1,000	$ 10,437
37	0	$ 26,969	$ 1,000	$ 12,581
38	0	$ 29,666	$ 1,000	$ 14,939
39	0	$ 32,633	$ 1,000	$ 17,533
40	0	$ 35,896	$ 1,000	$ 20,386
41	0	$ 39,486	$ 1,000	$ 23,525
42	0	$ 43,435	$ 1,000	$ 26,978
43	0	$ 47,779	$ 1,000	$ 30,776
44	0	$ 52,557	$ 1,000	$ 34,954
45	0	$ 57,813	$ 1,000	$ 39,549
46	0	$ 63,594	$ 1,000	$ 44,604
47	0	$ 69,953	$ 1,000	$ 50,164
48	0	$ 76,948	$ 1,000	$ 56,280
49	0	$ 84,643	$ 1,000	$ 63,008
50	0	$ 93,107	$ 1,000	$ 70,409
51	0	$102,418	$ 1,000	$ 78,550
52	0	$112,660	$ 1,000	$ 87,505
53	0	$123,926	$ 1,000	$ 97,356
54	0	$136,319	$ 1,000	$108,192
55	0	$149,951	$ 1,000	$120,111
56	0	$164,946	$ 1,000	$133,282
57	0	$181,441	$ 1,000	$147,644
58	0	$199,585	$ 1,000	$163,508
59	0	$219,544	$ 1,000	$180,959
60	0	$241,498	$ 1,000	$200,155

61	0	$265,648	$ 1,000	$221,271
62	0	$292,213	$ 1,000	$244,498
63	0	$321,434	$ 1,000	$270,048
64	0	$353,577	$ 1,000	$298,153
65	0	$388,935	$ 1,000	$329,068
Total	$8,000	$388,935	$36,000	$329,068

Here's another scenario to consider: If your child saves just one dollar a day from birth on, invested at an average of 12 percent compounded monthly for sixty-five years, his investment will become $7,181,410. That's what happens to only $23,430 when it is exposed to growth through compound interest. Let your mind think on that for a few minutes. Saving one dollars a day is not out of reach for most families. Of course, you would accumulate this and invest monthly or annually. One word of friendly advice: Start now!

Teaching your kids about compound interest

Here is a great story to tell your kids that will illustrate the miracle of compound interest.

In 1492 Christopher Columbus decided he was going to save for retirement. He had one penny ($0.01) and he knew he could earn 6 percent every year on his money. He put the penny in his left pocket and placed the interest ($0.01 x 6% = $0.0006) into his right pocket for safekeeping. He never added anything to his original penny in his left pocket. Yet the interest accumulated year after year in his right pocket.

Chris is a very healthy guy: He lives until today, 1998—506 years later—and exactly two years ago he decided to retire. So he took his one penny from his left pocket and added it to the simple interest in his right pocket. Do you know how much Mr. Columbus had?

Well, the interest in his right pocket added up to only $0.30 (504 years x $0.0006 = $.30). Along with his original penny from his left pocket he has $0.31 on which to retire. Not very good planning!

What could Chris have done differently? Let's assume Chris was much more astute about investing because he knew about compounding. Instead of putting the interest in his right pocket, he put it into his left pocket with the original penny—the principal. Over the years he would earn the same 6 percent interest on the original penny and the accumulated interest in his left pocket.

At the end of year one he had $0.0106 in his left pocket (the original penny plus the 6 percent interest). At the end of year two he had $0.011236 ($0.0106 plus 6 percent interest.) At the end of year three he had $0.01191 ($0.011236 plus 6 percent interest). This is called compounding and continued for Chris for 504 years. How much did good ol' Chris finally accumulate for retirement?

The answer is somewhat more to Chris's liking. At the end of 504 years of compounding the original penny at 6 percent interest, Chris has $56,774,862,806 (that's 56 *billion, 774 million,* 862 thousand, 806 dollars!) That's a lot of pocket change.

None of us will live that long, but all of us will have more than one penny to invest and will have the ability to compound our savings and investments at higher rates of return.[1]

The least they need to know about compound interest:

1. Compound interest makes your savings and investments grow. It is important to leave money alone so it can grow. If you withdraw it the growth stops.

2. Compound interest is like a teammate that you can always count on. Twenty-four hours a day, seven days a week it is earning money for you. It works weekends, holidays and nights. It never takes a day off and it earns just as much for you on the days when you are sick as when you are well.

Chapter 12

Neutralize the
Glamour of Credit

— $\$$ —

There is no reasonable way to shield your children
from the glitz and glamour of easy credit. It's everywhere, with all its seduction and allure. So if you cannot
shield, neutralize!

Years ago I watched an effective television documen
tary where juvenile delinquents went into prisons, drug-
treatment centers, and the like to observe the dark side of
the life they were heading toward. The intention was to
scare them out of their wits—to scare them straight.

In the same way these kids were jolted by reality, you
can scare your kids out of a life of consumer debt by reveal-
ing the lies behind the glamour.

As you know by now, I don't believe teenagers should
use credit cards, nor should they see the use of credit as a
viable way to live on a day-by-day basis. But kids don't
need to experience credit and debt first-hand to learn about
it. They don't need to own a credit card to understand every

last line of small print on a credit card application and the way the industry works.

Think of consumer credit as a stalker on the loose that is after kids. You know this stalker is out there, you know what he looks like, how he operates, and when he's most likely to strike. Your best line of defense is to describe him in detail to your kids and tell them everything you know about him so they can be prepared with a counter attack.

COLLECT STORIES

There is nothing so effective as true stories when it comes to scaring kids about the dangers of consumer debt. You've read a few such letters in this book. There are, unfortunately, thousands more where those came from.

From time to time you'll read stories in newspapers or magazines about how individuals and families have gone nuts with credit. I have drawers full of such clippings that tell of ruined lives.

Both Jeremy and Josh have worked in our newsletter publishing office over the years and that has given them plenty of opportunities to read some horror stories, but also some success stories, about consumer debt. It's difficult to work in the *Cheapskate Monthly* office without getting a consumer-debt wake-up call.

Share credit horror stories with your kids as often as you can (it's probably best to stick to stories you read in newspapers, newsletters, or other published sources rather than gossip). Let your teen or older child draw conclusions and suggest what would have been a better course of action. Let them be the ones to point out how foolish it is to live beyond your means. Then follow up with an explanation that when people aren't financially knowledgeable, they're easy marks for the trap of debt.

Real-life horror stories of consumer-credit-gone bad speak for themselves. It takes little follow-up to drive home the point that it's just not worth it to get into debt.

COLLECT CREDIT CARD APPLICATIONS

Those credit card applications that fill your mailbox make great teaching material. Have a few handy when an opportunity arises to go over them with your older kids and teens.

Using critical analysis, assess everything about each mailing piece: the envelope copy, the letter inside, the greeting, the promises, the flattery.

Move to the small print. These days the small print brings new meaning to "small," and many companies have gone to pale gray ink for the small print, making it even more difficult to read. It would be worth your time to have a few of these applications enlarged on a photocopy machine so you can easily read what they say.

Have your kids highlight all the lies and phrases of flattery they can find in the letters and credit card applications. Check the envelope too. Explain that it's human nature to enjoy this kind of praise, but it's wrong to use flattery to manipulate.

Search out all the statements that aren't true and challenge them. Example: "The more you spend, the more you'll save!" Truth: You cannot save by spending. The more you spend, the more you spend!

How about this one, "Use our credit card at any of the over 271,000 ATM machines and you'll have the cash you need!" Truth: Taking a cash advance on a credit card represents a very, very expensive loan. That really means you'll end up with more *debt* than you know!

Notice how many applications use words like spending limit, cash, power, prestige, unique services, privilege, and "you deserve." Notice the clever use of precious metals to make us think certain credit cards are more elegant which must mean we're more elegant to be invited to accept them. First there was just plain, then silver, gold, platinum. The latest is titanium.

Here are excerpts from the ten applications we received at our house in just one week (notice how they drip with flattery and manipulation):

- We want your business now! We want you to carry our most exclusive credit card because you've earned it with your excellent credit record.
- Every bank with a premium card wants your business. But we want it more! You'll be able to spend as you please! Your satisfaction guaranteed! This is just our way of thanking you for your business.
- You are pre-qualified! You're invited to request the card that reflects the financial standing you've achieved.

- Why settle for an ordinary credit card when you can request [name of card] which gives you the power, prestige, and acceptance you deserve?
- Because privilege speaks for itself, because you've earned it! Your success and accomplishments deserve recognition.
- Indeed there is no better value on the market today for financially savvy individuals like you. Due to your superior record of financial management, your excellent financial standing will be reflected in exceptional purchasing power.
- Travel and shop with the security of [name of card]. These privileges are simply not available to everyone. So it should come as no surprise that you are in a position to enjoy the very best we have to offer!

Go through your applications with your child and find all the times the word "debt" is used. (You could safely offer a ten-dollar reward for each occurrence your kids can find without having to worry much. The word debt is mysteriously missing from credit card applications.) Credit card applications make it appear that carrying a balance from month to month is some kind of benefit or privilege.

Talk about the interest rates, the late and over-limit fees, the terms under which the rules can be changed.

If you have access to a financial calculator (there are many credit card calculators on the Internet) or a computer program such as Quicken, play around with "what-ifs" using the terms of your credit card applications.

"What if I used this credit card to buy _____,
for $_____ and made the minimum payments
required? How many years would I be in debt and how
much interest would I end up paying?"

This is such an amazing exercise you'll secretly thank
the credit card companies for sending such effective anti-
debt teaching tools.

Once you've finished tearing apart the phony flattery
and exposing the truth of your application, don't throw it in
the trash. I have a better idea to help you and your kids put
a fun close on your critical examination.

Find the pre-addressed, postage-paid envelopes that
always accompany these offers and set them aside. Now
tear all the paper that came with it into tiny pieces and load
it back into the envelope. Seal it and send it back to the company. That is a good way to say "No, thank you!"

Never miss an opportunity to expose the danger of
credit card debt to your children.

Expose the Nothing-Nothing-Nothing Mystery

Perhaps you've wondered about the currently popular
"Nothing Down, No Payments, No Interest" kind of advertising. You'll see this in newspaper ads and store windows,
particularly around the holidays. What a seductive, yet
deceitful come-on! You must carefully read the fine print to
figure this out, and even then it can be confusing. I was so
curious I actually went into one of these stores advertising

such a "wonderful" opportunity and asked the credit manager to explain it to me.

First, there is a qualifying process. Only those customers with pristine credit reports can qualify. Next, the offer is for a limited time. Those "No Payments" are for the first six months or until January of next year—something like that. The customer must sign the credit application promising to pay some outrageous interest rate (usually the maximum allowed by state law which can be as high as 28 to 32 percent!), but the interest is deferred for the initial period. And here's the kicker: If the customer doesn't pay the entire amount due within that deferred interest period (and not one minute late according to the credit manager), interest becomes due immediately and it is retroactive to the date of purchase.

Here's the reason stores love to advertise this way: Most people who buy on credit don't have pristine credit so they can't qualify. But the "nothing" advertisement caught their attention and they'll probably fall for a more expensive deal. Of the people who do qualify for the no-no-no program, at least 78 percent fail to make the entire payment by the deadline, so they end up having to pay all that high interest back to day one.

This kind of nothing-down offer is very lucrative for the store because it gets a lot of people to come in. When only a small percentage can qualify for the no-no-no offer, they shuffle the rest into some other credit plan that nets the store even more money. There are lots of people out there who will do most anything to get something right now as long as they can pay for it later.

Whenever you see this kind of advertising, you can create a teachable moment by asking one of your kids how they think that works. "If you owned that store would you be worried about letting anyone take a house full of furniture with nothing down, no interest, and no payments?"

EXPOSE THE MYSTERY OF THE 125 PERCENT MORTGAGE

Even though this one isn't consumer credit (a mortgage loan is a secured loan) it is so outrageous it deserves to be exposed. Here's the scoop. Companies agree to loan you more than your home is worth. This is especially appealing to homeowners who have very little equity but need to get their hands on cash. The advertisements are compelling— "you'll have money to pay your debts, go on the vacation you deserve, add-on a family room" and on and on. The fine print reveals the horrendous terms. Some of these loans charge as much as 15 percent as a loan origination fee, or points (though a typical loan fee is 1 to 2 percent), and the interest rate is way above the going rates. The result is an outrageously high monthly payment.

If the mortgage company forecloses because the homeowner just couldn't keep up with the huge payments (it does make one wonder if that might be the motivation behind these lopsided loans), the lender gets the property plus all the interest they've collected. And don't forget that amazingly high loan origination fee of many thousands of dollars. These 125 percent loans can prove devastating for homeowners who don't understand the whole truth.

Never miss an opportunity to strike up a conversation about 125 percent real estate loans with your kids.

DE-GLAMORIZE HOME SHOPPING

Here's a great way to get your older kids to think realistically about the home shopping clubs on television. Start with a credit card application from your mailbox. Have your child figure out the terms. Now pretend that all of you will be going on a shopping spree with this phony-baloney credit card. Tune into one of the home shopping clubs and go wild! The rule is you can "buy" whatever you see but only for a pre-determined period of time. Write everything down that you've "ordered" with your pretend card. At the end of the time, add up the total cost plus the shipping and handling of all the junk you ordered. Now get your financial calculator and assess the "damage."

Using the total as the balance and the payment terms on the application, find out how many years it is going to take you to pay for this shopping spree. Whew! You'll be mighty glad this was only a game. And just think of all the junk you won't have to take care of.

Take a look at what I "bought" in only twenty minutes when I went on this kind of phony shopping spree:

Item	Price	S/H
16 piece gem set	$ 111.46	5.99
14K ring setting	$ 244.08	7.99

Shoe laces (3 pairs)	$ 11.87	3.97
Pearl leaf bracelet	$ 170.00	4.97
18K cherub charm bracelet	$ 704.50	4.97
Praying angel ring	$ 147.50	4.97
Fleur-de-lis 18K necklace	$ 422.00	4.97
18K angel pendant	$ 56.25	3.97
18K lady with orchids necklace	$2154.00	9.97
18K cross pendant	$ 65.00	3.97
18K gold cable chain	$ 397.00	5.97
Nine-inch 18K anklet	$ 186.00	4.97

I bought $4,735 in shopping club stuff of marginal quality in twenty minutes. Pretending that I put this on a 18.99 percent interest credit card that requires minimum payments of 3 percent of the outstanding balance (or ten dollars whichever is more), here is the damage I did in just twenty minutes: It would take more than nineteen years (234 months) of minimum monthly payments to pay back a total of $9,793, including interest.

EXPOSE THE REAL NUMBERS ON MUSIC CLUBS

The advertisements are very tempting. What kid these days wouldn't be interested in getting ten music CDs for ten cents? While many of these kinds of music and book clubs offer an excellent service to mature adults, kids have a difficult time seeing through the promise of something for nothing.

Take a few of the club offerings and enlarge them on a photocopy machine so you and the kids can easily read all the tiny print. Here's what kids need to know: Even though the initial order is really inexpensive (nearly free!) there's usually a significant shipping and handling fee per book or per CD. That fee per item is often about the same it would cost to by a similar product in a discount store. But the kicker is that by accepting that initial offer, you agree to the terms of the club. Sometimes you are obligated to a buy a certain number of selections at the full price. Making it even more difficult for kids, some of these clubs have what is called a "negative response" feature. By accepting that initial offer you have agreed to purchase the monthly selection and you'll receive it every month along with a bill for the full price plus shipping and handling—unless you are careful to return the card that says you don't want it

All of these things should make mail order music and books clubs off limits for kids. By saving their money and watching for sales, kids can generally beat the club prices, even taking into consideration the initial offering, and get just the titles they really want.

The best way to neutralize the glamour of consumer credit is to face it head-on and expose it! Talking openly and honestly with your kids about the pitfalls will remove the hard candy shell to reveal the bitter pill beneath.

Chapter 13
The Preschool Years

— $\$$ —

C hildren under the age of five don't possess the cognitive skills necessary to make a connection between money and value. In fact, preschoolers have little, if any, understanding of money at all.

They don't understand the theory behind saving because they have no concept of time. They much prefer a nickel to a dime because it's bigger.

While attempting to teach abstract financial ideas to children so young would be of little benefit, it is of huge importance to understand that during the first five years of life a child develops much of his or her moral intelligence.

Kids are shaped at the very beginning of life by the way their parents live. They are ever-attentive witnesses to grown-up behaviors. They take their cues from what they see and hear. What they do best is observe and imitate.

While they don't understand the meaning of abstract ideas, even toddlers can learn frugality by seeing that we are not wasteful, and that we are thankful for what we have. Children grow morally by learning how to be with others and how to behave in the world.

If you want your children to grow up with healthy attitudes about money, and what it can and cannot do, start demonstrating those attitudes and behaviors from day one.

"DO'S" FOR PRESCHOOLERS

Let them observe that Mommy and Daddy have money and they take good care of it.

Let them see their parents and older siblings use money as an ordinary and normal part of life.

Let them see you put money in the church offering. Make sure they catch you being generous with others and sharing what you have.

Tell your kids stories about the times God takes care of you.

Let them see you deposit money in the bank.

Let them see the way you pay for groceries with cash.

Teach them that money is important in our lives because we can exchange it for things we need and want.

Talk about money as casually as you talk about other things like sports and laundry.

Take every opportunity during these formative years to instill in your children a genuine faith in God.

Use coins to teach your preschooler to count. It's effective and acknowledges their curiosity about money.

Talk about the different shapes and colors of items in

the store. It gives little ones something to do instead of wanting everything they see.

Allow your little one while riding in the grocery cart to hold the coupons or the list. Talk about finding the best value.

Say "we don't choose to spend our money that way" more often than you say "we can't afford it."

Remember preschoolers are listening and learning from everything they see you do and hear you say.

Use coins to teach the different denominations. Three- and four-year-olds can learn to put all the pennies into one cup, the nickels into another, and so on.

Visit the library and park with your preschooler more often than the market or mall.

Give rewards of hugs and praise—not money. Creating the expectation of cash payment at every turn is a habit you'll regret in adolescence.

Monitor television time and opt for non-commercial viewing and videotapes when possible.

Let preschoolers participate in household chores to enjoy the security of belonging—not to get paid.

Intervene between advertisers and your kids. Pre-schoolers can't always tell when the television show ends and the ad begins.

Make sure your children grow up knowing that all good things are a blessing from God.

Let your children count potatoes, oranges, and other items as you put them in the bag at the grocery store.

"Don'ts" for Preschoolers

Don't confuse children's healthy attitudes about real money by using credit cards and ATM machines when they're around.

Don't argue about money in front of the kids.

Don't allow preschoolers to be only takers. Help them find ways to give to others.

Don't overindulge your preschoolers. It's healthy for them to yearn just a little from time to time. It will help prepare them for real life when they cannot have everything they want.

Don't use money to bribe or manipulate. Kids pick up on that quickly.

Don't let your child see or hear you worry about money.

Don't let your kids mistake love for money. Little surprises and gifts of money are expressions of affection, but very young children see them as substitutes.

Don't overexpose toddlers and preschoolers to stores and supermarkets.

Don't forget that too much commercial television creates unhealthy doses of desire.

Don't be surprised if despite your best efforts your preschoolers still want it all. It's natural. Young kids forget quickly what they didn't get—but ugly attitudes of entitlement go on and on.

"It is by his deeds that a lad distinguishes himself if his conduct is pure and right. The hearing ear and the seeing eye, the Lord has made both of them" (Proverbs 20:11–12, NASB).

Chapter 14
Six through Nine

— $\$$ —

B y now your children have moved into their elementary school years. They are reading; they understand simple abstract ideas. But that's not all. They have become part of that important demographic group of kiddy consumers we mentioned in chapter 7—kids who will determine how more than $141 billion will be spent on them in this year alone. An entire industry is focusing its attention on your kids. They have become very much a part of the real world.

MAKE AN ALLOWANCE

Most six-year-olds these days know about allowances, but it doesn't stop there. They want their own money too. You might be able to put them off for a few more years—even until they are old enough to go into a formal salary program like our HKFP (see chapter 4). But why wait if they are ready for some hands-on learning now? A simple allowance program will fit perfectly into these interim years before they are ready to go on salary.

Think of it this way: If putting your children on salary when they are older will be like swimming in the deep end, then giving them an allowance now will let them in the shallow end of the pool—complete with water wings, swimming lessons, and you, their attentive lifeguards.

At this age kids are teachable, eager to learn, and they still believe everything adults tell them. You will have wonderful opportunities to pass on your values to your elementary-aged kids as you closely guide them through simple lessons on needs versus wants, giving, and saving for future purchases.

How much and how often?

The exact allowance amount will depend on your particular situation. As you are deciding on a figure, remember you want these years to be an understated precursor of what is to come when your kids' ages are double-digits and they go on salary.

Some families set allowances according to age—fifty cents to one dollar for each year of age. That method automatically determines when and how much to increase.

At this age, kids do better with close supervision and short time frames so receiving their allowance weekly is best. Set a specific day of the week to pay allowances so everyone knows what to expect—no surprises, no misunderstandings.

Tied to chores?

Many experts say absolutely yes—allowance should be the payment children receive for doing their chores and assigned jobs. No work? No pay. They say the allowance must be earned.

Other experts feel that as citizens of the "family community," where each family member has the right to share in its rewards, income, and responsibilities, allowances should be the child's share of the family income. They say an allowance should not be the payment for chores and assigned jobs. But, they add, with privilege comes responsibility. Citizens must do chores and jobs because they are part of the community—not for payment. That's just what good citizens do.

I go with the second group. Children learn responsibility when they perform chores that are commensurate with their age and abilities. But they're still kids. And they will forget or do an unacceptable job now and then. It's unfair to dock their pay or withhold their allowance. Handle the matter in a way that fits the infraction.

A third allowance alternative would be to combine all of these options. Give your kids a base allowance that is quite low and assign them regular chores that are separate from the allowance. Then post a list of optional jobs that are available for additional pay, ET=EM (extra tasks equal extra money). Example: Wash Mom's car—$5.00. This variation on the allowance-versus-chores-theme seems to cover all the bases. The children can count on a portion of the community income, they are responsible to work for the community, and they have an incentive to earn more money when they have the time and one of those posted jobs looks interesting.

You will recall from a previous chapter we did not dock or withhold from our kids' salaries if they failed to do their chores or did them unacceptably. We gave them citations and the greater the offense, the higher the fine. Like getting a speeding ticket, it's a painful way to learn a lesson.

WHAT ABOUT GIVING AND SAVING?

Your kids need to begin living the values you're teaching them about giving first and then always saving part of all the money they receive. Enforcing these values through the allowance system gets those values operating in their lives from a very young age.

Jars are popular with kids this age and become perfect substitutes for bank accounts. In one family each child has four jars marked to show the deposit allocations:

Giving:	10 percent
Long-term savings:	30 percent
Short-term savings:	30 percent
Spend now:	30 percent

Their plan says that long-term savings is for college or something far away. Short-term savings is for something significant like a new bike or toy and "spend now" is money the child can spend right away.

Another family has a community Giving Jar. Everyone puts 10 percent in the central collection center, and then each person has a jar, similar to the plan above. When the Giving Jar accumulates a tidy sum they call a Community Meeting to present ideas of where to give the money. Then the family votes and makes the delivery.

COMMUNITY TAXES

There's no time like when they're young to teach kids about taxes. I think this is a clever idea, one every family should consider. The community levies taxes on its citizens. The family I heard about voted for a 15 percent tax across the board. Every person on allowance has their taxes withheld and deposited directly to the Tax Jar. The family voted the tax revenues would go toward the family vacation—a representative democracy in action.

SPENDING

While your kids should have some portion of their allowance to spend as they decide, they also need supervision. Some parents require a written account of some kind—at the very least, permission to make purchases.

Kids should have a clear understanding of family values regarding what they can buy and what's not allowed in their home. One family wrote that a daughter used her spending money to buy a tube top—something that was clearly not acceptable. She lost the garment and her money on that poor choice. You'll especially want to monitor your younger children's spending closely.

ONCE IT'S GONE, IT'S GONE

It's important that you absolutely not allow your children to borrow money. Not even for five minutes until you get home from the store. Remember the title of this book. If they spend their money, that's their choice. But there's no more until next allowance day. Your kids will never learn to be confident money managers if they just get more when they run out. An "advance" on next week's allowance is another way to say "debt."

UNIQUE PRODUCTS

I have come across two unique products I like so much I want you to know about them.

ParentBanc Jr. This product introduces young children to banking and money management using an innovative idea that works like a regular checking account. Parents act as bankers and their children are the customers. As children receive money for gifts or allowance, they "deposit" it with their parents and keep track of the balance in their ParentBanc register. When children want cash they write a check to their parents. This creates an opportunity for communication between parent and child while helping to account for children's expenditures. The ParentBank Jr. New Account Kit comes with a checkbook cover, colorful kid's checks, picture ID Card, real calculator, wide-ruled check register, and instructional guide. This could replace jars and work well for older children in this age group. I bought this item at a toy store for about eight dollars. (See resources.)

American Girls Savings Game. If you have a girl aged eight to twelve you have likely heard of the American Girls Collection. The company sells a rather pricey line of quality dolls, books, and all kinds of accessories. Each doll represents a period in American history, so there's an educational aspect. This company also developed the American Girls Savings Game. The object of the game is to complete a jigsaw puzzle of the American Girls by earning twenty puzzle-piece stickers. You earn stickers by saving money. When you save the money and earn all the stickers you will have finished the puzzle—and have enough money saved to buy the item you want from the collection. The game requires the girl to select a savings coach to encourage and monitor the savings. It teaches the girl to set her goal (including the purchase price, shipping and handling, and tax), then shows her how to divide that number by the amount of money she wishes to save. The girl can see immediately how long it will take her to save for the purchase.

One young friend of mine was hot to "play the game" so she could get an item she just couldn't live without. However, once she saw in black and white exactly how many months this project was going to take—and how much cash it would cost—she changed her mind.

The game, while specific to this particular company and its products, is a wonderful model for teaching kids to save for a specific item. Free of charge, the American Girl Savings Game is well worth a toll-free phone call. (See resources.)

Chapter 15
Ten through Teen

— $\$$ —

They want independence and freedom. You want them to take responsibility for their actions. They want decision-making power. You want them to make the right choices. They are struggling to break away. You can't bear the thought of letting go. Welcome to adolescence.

It has been nearly fifteen years since we designed our HKFP plan (chapters 4 and 5). We have had plenty of time to evaluate and the results are in. In all its simplicity, our plan was successful. I mean hugely, wonderfully successful. The plan accomplished its purpose. We put our kids in charge of their own spending decisions. We gave them a significant salary, lots of financial responsibility, and stepped back into the position of advisors, even as we were getting our own financial house in order.

Things are different now than they were in the mid-1980s when we took Uncle Harvey's idea and developed it into a unique money plan for our family. Consumer credit wasn't so available then as it is now—especially to teens and young adults. We would have thought the Internet was something you attached between two trees to make a hammock. The commercialization of our lives was not so intense.

Still, I know that our financial plan—because it is so simple, logical, and adaptable to any parent-child situation—can do for your family what it did for ours. This is a reasonable way to eliminate the power-struggles that clog the channels of communication between teens and their parents.

If your children have been on an allowance system, moving into a salaried plan will be the next logical step. But if not, and your kids are new to any kind of allowance program or financial responsibility, don't hesitate to jump in now and get them up to speed. It is at this point in our kids' lives—age 10 or 11—that we recommend beginning our plan. It's only too late if you don't start now, no matter what your pre-teen or teen's age.

A Written Plan

I have a theory about plans. If it's not written down, it's only a dream. You don't want your kids' financial futures floating around in some dream state. That's why your kids' financial plan should be a written document. There are other benefits to writing your plan:

- it becomes visually symbolic;
- it creates authority;
- it organizes your ideas and values; and
- it will give your kids something to show their kids (think family heirloom).

Equipment. This can be as simple or elaborate as you want but before you run out and spend a fortune on some leather-bound portfolio, remember you can always upgrade later. All you need in the beginning is a notebook and paper. A three-ring binder, a scrap book, or a photo album could be adapted quite easily.

Plan book sections. Divide your plan book into sections for the mission statement, various provisions, rules regarding salaries, mandatory giving, saving, spending, raises, and responsibilities. You'll also want a section for each of your children where you can record their yearly responsibility lists and salary histories. I'm sure there are as many ways to set this up as there are families. The only way you can get it wrong is if you don't try.

Mission statement. Develop a written statement that describes the purpose of your plan and how you intend to accomplish it.

Writing a mission statement is a powerful process. It takes all those ideas floating around in your head and turns them into something clear and useful. Developing your own unique purpose in this simple way will create a sense of excitement and adventure. It might take a few minutes; it could take weeks.

THE BASIC PLAN PROVISIONS

Responsibility list. This is a detailed list of all the items that you will no longer buy for your child. The ten-year-olds' list should be quite different from someone who is seventeen. The theory is you keep adding responsibilities so that by the last year on the plan, the child's list includes everything, with the possible exception of at-home food and shelter.

Salary. This is the sum of money you give to your child that covers all the items you would normally buy for him and which are on the responsibility list.

Payment method. Salary should be paid on a monthly basis in cash. It requires more responsibility and demands the child to make better plans if it comes less often but in a larger quantity. And it seems like a more serious amount of money. Twenty-five dollars a week is not as dramatic as one hundred dollars a month.

Mandatory disbursements. Our rule was that all salaried individuals must give and save. You can hardly go wrong by following the classic 10-10-80 formula (10 percent to be given away, 10 percent to savings, leaving 80 percent to live on).

Spending. We allowed our boys to make their own spending decisions for 80 percent of their salary. The first year all the items on their responsibility list were "wants." There was nothing that they had to buy, but if they wanted anything on that list, they used their money. As your children grow and the lists (and salaries) expand you will likely add clothes, haircuts, and school supplies, among a myriad of other things. While they are still making their decisions regarding spending for anything on the list, there should be a clear expectation that they will get haircuts and buy the required school supplies.

Record keeping. Kids must keep a written spending record and a spending plan (see chapter 11). We neglected to include this important rule in our plan and if we had it to do again, this would be mandatory. At the time we just didn't know how important it is to know where the money goes. Enforce this rule more for creating a life-long habit, not so much so the child becomes accountable to the parent for every nickel spent. The spending record becomes the budgeting tool and will be enormously important as kids begin buying their clothes.

Spending records will also become important if there is a complaint along the way that a child's responsibilities exceed his salary. Without a detailed record of where his money is going you won't know if there really is a discrepancy or simply an overspending problem.

Borrowing. Unless it's a matter of health or personal safety, there should be no salary advances or borrowing. As the debt-proof component to this entire matter of financial responsibility, loans are not an alternative. You want your plan as loophole-free as possible.

Graduation. Don't forget to decide when your salary plan will end. We continued through the summer after high school, but this would be a matter unique to each family's situation. Some families wean their kids off salary gradually as they begin to find employment outside the home.

Parental hands-off. Parents must pledge to follow the hands-off rule. This is the most difficult provision for the parents but one of the favorites of the kids. By letting your kids make their own spending decisions without your interference, you empower them with confidence. As a parent who's been there, let me tell you how difficult it will be to keep your mouth shut. But you must. Your kids will never learn the truth about consequences if they aren't allowed to make mistakes. Just be thankful they'll be making them while the consequences are not long-lasting or earth-shattering.

GETTING STARTED

The ideal time to put kids on salary is when they are young enough to be impressed but mature enough to reason and understand simple financial concepts. The ideal age seems to be about ten or eleven. When in doubt, sooner is better than later. It really is ideal to get kids started on a salary plan before they reach adolescence. Start while they are still compliant, think their parents are terrific, and don't talk back. They'll make the transition into adolescence so smoothly you'll wonder if everything is normal.

Explaining the system

Most kids are more than speechless when they learn about a family plan that will allow them to make their own spending decisions. When they hear how much money they will be managing they are eager to get going. It's important to stress it's not all privilege—a great deal of responsibility is expected. They need to know just how much trust is being placed in them, that you trust them to handle large sums of money and to make wise choices.

A starting salary

One reason you need to start planning many months in advance is so you know what you spend on your kids. Trust me, you'll be amazed, because as it dribbles out of your pockets and purses it doesn't seem like much. Just start keeping track. Even with all of this information, you'll still have to estimate and finally just pick a number. But at least you'll be in the right ballpark.

Once you get a few years down the road, the monthly salary is going to be significant. If you add up all the clothes, cosmetics, haircuts, yearbooks, movies, school supplies, gifts, gasoline, dates, sports, lessons, trips, books, CDs, and on and on that you buy for your kids and teens in the course of a year, you're looking at a substantial number. Divide that by twelve and it's not unthinkable that an older teen's monthly salary will be $150, $200, or even more, depending on your lifestyle and situation. It is important that you be as realistic as possible in estimating your kids' expenses.

THE LAUNCH

Going on salary is a very important step for a kid—a rite of passage. If you treat the event in a memorable way it will take on even more significance. A special dinner or certificate can imprint the start of this new season as each of your children become full-fledged family money managers.

ANNUAL EXPANSION

At least once a year (more often if your kids are older when they start) sit down with your child and add as many more items to their responsibility lists as possible. As you add more and more things to the list, more responsibility is required, and more learning will happen. By the time you reach the senior year of high school, salaries should be at a level to cover all senior expenses such as class rings, prom, yearbooks, and senior trips. You can see how tricky this can get.

Clearly this is not a one-size-fits-all-families kind of money plan. There are so many variables. But the basic plan is adaptable to all situations.

Q & A

Everyone who hears about this kind of plan for the first time has questions. Here are some of the most frequently asked:

Q: I can't imagine giving my ten-year-old fifty dollars and expecting him to know what to do with it, let alone have anything left next week at this time.

A: Of course you wouldn't do that without a great deal of preparation (chapter 4) and some very clear-cut rules. At age ten your son may not be mature enough to jump in at this more advanced level. Why not put him into more structured allowance program (see chapter 14) for a year or so, where he receives a weekly allowance with fewer responsibilities and more supervision?

Q: Doesn't this salary program constitute a free hand-out that will only encourage kids to turn into adults who think they don't have to work for a living?

A: No. If you've read all the chapters you know I believe children should do chores and regular work around the house, not for pay but because they are citizens of the family community. I believe that children are their parents' financial responsibility. While some think that kids need to get outside jobs to pay for things they want, I don't agree. I believe childhood is a time to learn about life, not to be employed. Kids need to be kids, to participate fully in school and become educated. We didn't keep it a secret with our boys that they would be expected to get jobs in the summer of their senior year in high school. They had plenty of notice for when their salaries would end. There were no complaints, no problems. They both got their jobs, we stopped paying salaries, and the transition was seamless. They were pleased because the salaries we were giving them were far less than what they earned on their part-time jobs. Our salary structure did not allow for a lavish lifestyle. Actually, it taught our boys to be quite frugal. The salary we turned over to them was the same money we had used to buy things for them. We simply transferred the money from our care into theirs.

Q: Our son is twelve. We like for him to go to church camp twice a year. If we include the cost of camp in his salary, does he get to choose whether to go or not?

A: That's the way the plan works. If this was a case where he was eager to go, you wouldn't have a problem. But if he's going because you make him go, you'd better not include that in the salary. By you paying for his camp you retain control over him in that area. When we faced the camp situation with Josh, he wanted to go to camp as badly as we wanted him to go. But camp was a little pricey and his salary was none-too-extravagant. We compromised by matching his contribution, which means we paid half, but only if he really went. We didn't simply increase his salary by the amount we were willing to pay. As a rule of thumb, parents should pay for anything they wish to keep under their control.

Q: What if you have a child who is so money hungry he stops spending money at all and just sits home all the time.

A: If you are going to trust your kids to participate in this kind of program, you must accept their decisions. Personally, I don't think this would go on for long and you may be simply anticipating something that will never happen. For sure, there will be some extreme behaviors in the beginning. But it will level out. Keep a journal so you'll be able to remember the stories.

Q: I think it's too risky to give my son this kind of latitude. What if he takes all his money and buy cigarettes with it, or worse?

A: If that is your worry, you have something other than a salary problem. Putting your kids on this kind of salary or an allowance program (chapter 14) isn't going to create rebellious behavior. If that behavior is already in place, you need to deal with it before proceeding with this kind of problem.

Q: Isn't it a little rigid to say "no borrowing"? Kids are kids and if they don't have enough money or forgot to bring it with them to the store, shouldn't we cut them a little slack?

A: I say no. The point of this program is to get your kids ready for the real world. You wouldn't want your twenty-five-year-old daughter thinking that every time she didn't have any money in her purse, someone (Visa? MasterCard?) should cut her a little slack by giving her a loan, would you? Well, now's the time to teach that value. Your kids will not suffer long if they have to forego some item they really want or sit home a time or two.

Q: What if the family goes out for a movie? Does the child on salary have to pay for their own ticket?

A: That all depends on what your plan says. You should address those kinds of issues ahead of time. I'll tell you what we did. If we went to a movie for a family outing, we picked up the tab—it was our treat. And let me tell you that once your kids are on salary, they really appreciate things like Mom and Dad buying their movie ticket.

Q: My daughter is sixteen and has never had any kind of consistent money training. She's never received an allowance, and I feel badly about that. Is it too late?

A: Oh, no! But you have no time to lose. I suggest you read this book through again and then have her read it. This isn't difficult, especially for an older teen. I would start with a three-month plan. Set her up on a weekly allowance using chapter 14 as a guide. She'll pick it up quickly and you can move right to a more aggressive salary program.

Q: We tried this kind of a plan with our eleven-year-old daughter and it was a disaster. She spent all of her money foolishly in the first week. We held on for another week but decided she was just too young.

A: You can't expect your child to become a responsible money manager overnight. But you have to stick with it. You cannot supplement with more cash when they make mistakes. You want their biggest financial bloopers to happen early on when there is no harm that can come to them while they suffer. You must let your kids face and feel the consequences of their choices. They do learn eventually, and better they do that while they are at home and not a thousand miles away on a college campus with a credit card in tow.

Q: What about cars for teens? Who buys what?

A: No doubt about it, teens and cars go together these days. First there's the cost of the car and then the insurance, gasoline, and maintenance. There are many things to consider. Next, is this a "want" or a "need"? What are the alternatives? Is there a family car to share? You might consider a matching program. Or if the teen buys the car, agree to pay for the insurance. Or vice versa. Our boys both saved enough money from the time they were about ten years old to buy their cars in high school. We paid the insurance, but they covered all other expenses. Whether your teens have their own cars or share the family's, they need to share significantly in the costs or there will be little appreciation.

Q: When should a teen get a credit card, if ever?

A: I think the junior year in college is the ideal time. (It really is necessary for every adult to have one credit card to use as a tool. Graduating college students will need to show an active credit report to rent an apartment or get a job. Employers and landlords look at a credit history as a character reference.) By this time he or she is about twenty and as an enrolled college student can get a credit card without any problem, as you know. The good thing is that by the time your teen turns twenty and has been "debt-proofed," he or she will know exactly how to use that card as a tool, not a noose with which to hang himself.

If your freshman is going away to college and you feel he must have a credit card just for your peace of mind, you have several options: 1) You can add his name to your card. This way you will get the statement every month and know what's going on. Of course you might know after the fact, but you'll be within thirty days of any untoward activity. 2) You can cosign with him on a card in his name but request that the statements come to your address. In this case he will start his own credit history. 3) Have him get his own secured credit card in his name. He will have to put up a security deposit of about three hundred dollars that will earn interest (this should be his money too). Now the statements go to him at school, and he's responsible for how he uses the card. He cannot go over the three-hundred-dollar limit; and if he should for some reason, and fail to make the payment, they will use his three-hundred-dollar security deposit and close the account. If he does well, which I think he will, the account will convert to a regular unsecured account in two years, and he can get his deposit back with interest. I would go with the third option. This keeps his activity off your record and makes him responsible for his behavior.

Chapter 16
A Final Thought

— $$$ —

There's no doubt that the letting-go part of parenting isn't easy. But we can make the process easier and much more enjoyable if we keep this thought at the front of our minds: God's plan is for children to grow wings and fly away.

Our job as parents is to prepare them for the flight. Building financial confidence in your kids is one important way you can help them fly high above the turbulence with grace and endurance.

Write to me and let me know how those flying lessons are going!

Mary Hunt
P.O. Box 2135
Paramount, CA 90723-8135

Epilogue

— $\$$ —

You might wonder what has become of our boys. I will bring you up to date with just the facts and without going on and on about how great they are and what fine, responsible men they've become. And how proud we are of them. And how we're wondering if perhaps we should have added something to our plan that describes the process of actually leaving home one day. Thankfully we put in a pay-rent clause.

JEREMY HUNT

Jeremy is now twenty-four. His family salary ceased the end of the summer 1992. He worked part-time during college and graduated from California State University Long Beach in 1997, debt-free. He got a credit card during his junior year. He reports that he uses it occasionally as a tool but has never paid a nickel's worth of interest. He continues to be an amazing saver and lives well beneath his means.

Jeremy majored in film production and is now a digital effects artist for a company that does that kind of work for the television and film industry. If you are a Trekkie, it's likely you have seen his work.

JOSH HUNT

Josh is twenty-two. His family salary ceased at the end of summer 1994, however he had already secured a job so he had a rather lucrative few months. He worked part-time through school. He graduated debt-free from trade school in 1997 as a state certified locksmith. He works at a firm in Orange County.

Josh, too, is an amazing saver and is working on a fairly impressive investment portfolio. Josh still doesn't have a credit card, which isn't all that bad, but in these times he needs to break down and get one if for no other reason than to have an active credit file.

Josh lives way below his means. Money for him, or his brother for that matter, has never been an issue or a problem.

UNCLE HARVEY

Uncle Harvey died in 1993. Not long after, his son Paul and wife Sandra visited us in California. You can imagine how anxious I was to meet Uncle Harvey's youngest so we could compare notes. After all, Paul had grown up under the *original* Hunt Financial Program—the deluxe model from which we'd adapted our financial plan.

We were eager to share with Paul how we had customized his family's plan and passed it on through the lives of our sons. And you can believe I'd be taking notes. You just never know—maybe one day Paul and Sandra's kids would compare notes with our kids in order to help customize just the right plan for their kids. (Maybe they'd write a book.) We were about to experience a heritage moment.

I was nothing if not stunned when Paul responded to my opening question with a blank stare. The silence was deafening. Following what seemed like an eternity, he explained he'd never heard of such a thing, giving any kids—and certainly not him or his three brothers—all the money they would need for the entire year. All at once. In cash. You could have knocked me over with a feather and Harold would have fallen right behind.

I wasted little time writing to Aunt Rotha inquiring about the plan. I did feel badly questioning Paul, but it crossed my mind that maybe they did things so smoothly, and Paul being the youngest, he didn't realize he was on such a plan. It could happen.

Her response confirmed that Paul was right—we were way off base. The story we'd heard (and embellished beyond the legal limit I'm sure) was a legend, and not a very well-known one at that.

I couldn't believe it. We'd spent all these years shaping and designing our children's financial training only to learn our inspiration was nothing more than a legend.

Aunt Rotha wrote, "Regarding the allowances given to our boys, they had their chores to do to earn it—chores at the barn, milking the cows, and sending the milk to the factory each day thus receiving a monthly cheque, which they divided among themselves."

It was a hoax but we quickly realized that it didn't matter. Not a bit. In fact, had we not believed the story I doubt that we would have had the courage to take it and expand, develop, and customize it to fit our family uniquely.

I'm thankful we didn't attempt to confirm the details at the beginning of our journey. Had we known we were making it up as we went, we might have doubted our ability to carry through. Because we believed the trail had already been blazed we had the courage to follow.

Truly it was a faith journey.

Resources

— $\$$ —

I hope this book will be the catalyst that sends you in search of more information and ways for you and your kids to learn about money and right living.

Books for Parents

Swindoll, Charles R. *You and Your Child.* Nashville: Thomas Nelson Inc., Publishers, 1977. A biblical and practical guide to rearing children. It clearly sets down God's principles but allows each parent to work out those principles in terms of their children's own personalities. Most importantly, the book is permeated with the author's love of people, God, and his Word. Note: This book is currently out of print but well worth your time to find it. Try a church library or out-of-print bookstore.

Burkett, Larry and Rick Osborne. *Financial Parenting.* Colorado Springs, Colo.: Victor Books, 1996. Gives solid practical advice to parents on teaching their children biblical financial management. Authors give practical help, tips, and activities to teach kids basic money skills and management, using the Bible as the primary teaching tool.

Bodnar, Janet. *Kiplinger's Money-Smart Kids (And Parents, Too!)*. Washington D.C.: The Kiplinger Washington Editors, Inc., 1993. Addresses financial issues strictly for parents. Author shows how to identify your "money style," set limits, and reaffirm values you want to share with your children. Tackles pressing issues like saving for college, buying the right amounts and types of insurance, and providing for your children if you're not there.

Bodnar, Janet. *Mom, Can I Have That?* New York: Random House, 1996. The wise, warm, and witty Janet Bodnar, in her guise as Dr. Tightwad, tackles more than a hundred questions that kids ask most frequently about money (and your financial situation!).

Estess, Patricia Schiff and Irving Barocas. *Kids, Money, and Values,* Ohio: Betterway Books, 1994. Everyone wants to raise a child who turns into a financially responsible and mature adult. This book can help you reach that goal by teaching your children the importance of money management now. Or you can wait and bail them out when they're older and should know better. The choice is up to you.

Neale S. Godfrey, *A Penny Saved.* New York: Simon & Schuster, 1995. Shows parents how to teach their children about money: what it is, how it works, and how to use it effectively and responsibly. This book expands on these essential life lessons for kids from preschoolers through teens and gives parents a concrete structure to tech values and life skills.

Schor, Juliet B. *The Overspent American.* New York: Basic Books, 1998. More than a quarter of all families making more than $100,000 a year say they cannot afford to buy everything they need. Overall, half the population of the richest country in the world claims not to be able to afford the basics—and it's not just the poorer half. The book describes the growing backlash of people who are "downshifting" by working less, earning less, and finding balance by getting their lifestyles in sync with their values.

Blix, Jacqueline and David Heitmiller. *Getting a Life.* New York: Viking, 1997. A married couple explain how they gradually transformed their lives over the past six years. They left their fast-track lives—two corporate jobs, expensive cars, exotic trips, thoughtless overspending—for an existence that reflects their true values and life purpose. These self-styled "reformed yuppies" are joined by more than two dozen individuals and families of diverse backgrounds who share their own stories of frugality and fulfillment.

Tobias, Cynthia Ulrich. *The Way They Learn.* Colorado Springs, Colo.: Focus on the Family, 1996. Every person learns differently—and that can cause conflict, especially between parents and children. But it doesn't have to. Cynthia Tobias gives practical examples and valuable, easy-to-understand models to help moms and dads better understand the types of learning approaches that will work best for their children and help them do better in school.

BOOKS FOR KIDS

Burgeson, Nancy. *The Money Book for Kids.* New York: Troll Associates, 1992. A terrific 32-page book for kids ages seven to twelve. Includes several quizzes and games.

Berg, Adriane G. *The Totally Awesome Money Book for Kids and Their Parents.* New York: New Market Press, 1993. For kids ages ten to seventeen. Written by the author and her young son, this has some great sections on how kids can make money and begin investing. Caution: Chapters 16-17 on debt may not line up with your values on the subject.

Harris, Richard. *Who Taught You About Money?* Virginia Beach, Va.: Hampton Roads Publishing Company, 1994. Written in rhyme this is a fun book for kids ages seven to fourteen or to be read to younger children. Example: "Money by itself is neither good or is it bad, it's the way in which you choose to use it that brings joy or makes you sad." Put that to a rap beat and your kids will eat it up. Topics are extensive, including A Medium of Exchange, Attitude about Money, Taxes, Net Worth, Insurance. Very cleverly written.

Otfinsoski, Steve. *The Kid's Guide to Money.* New York: Scholastic Reference, 1996. Excellent and complete money guide for kids ages nine and up. Presents consumer debt pretty well, but leaves the door open. Read chapter 5 with your child.

BOOKS FOR TEENS

Temple, Todd. Money: *How to Make It, Spend It, and Keep Lots of It.* Nashville: Broadman & Holman Publishers, 1998. By far my favorite book on the subject matter for teens. The author, a former youth minister and author of many books for teens, offers a biblical perspective and knows how to communicate with teens.

Kobliner, Beth. *Get a Financial Life,* New York: Fireside, 1996. Written from the world's perspective, you'll want to approach this work with caution. Excellent financial content for advanced teens through twenty-somethings. Tolerant of consumer and student debt. Excellent resource for a young person who just landed that first big job in the real world.

Palow, Sally. *Cool Cash: Economics & Money for Kids.* Grand Rapids, Mich.: TS Denison, 1996. This sixteen-page booklet has an entrepreneurial flavor directed at kids ages ten to sixteen. May be difficult to find. Beneficial for the eager entrepreneur.

BOOKS FOR PARENTS OF TEENS

Hahn, Dr. Daniel. *Teaching Your Kids the Truth About Consequences.* Minneapolis, Minn.: Bethany House Publishers, 1995. This isn't another book about discipline or theory but a practical plan for parents who want to help kids develop an internal compass for living in a world where Christian principles are questioned and even scorned. Financial matters are not the focus, although the author uses money situations as examples.

A Parent's Guide: Advertising and Your Child. Brochure. The Children's Advertising Review Unit (CARU) was established by the advertising industry to promote responsible children's advertising and to respond to public concerns. CARU publishes this guide which discusses how you can monitor and explain advertising to your children. To order contact CARU, 845 Third Ave,. New York, NY 10022, (212) 705-0124.

OTHER TEACHING RESOURCES

ParentBanc Jr. This product introduces young children to banking and money management using an innovative idea that works like a regular checking account. Parents act as bankers and their children are the customers. Check your local toy store or ParentBanc®, 44 East Avenue, Suite 201, Austin, TX 78701, (800) 471 3000.

American Girls Savings Game. The game is a wonderful
model for teaching kids to save for a specific item
and an excellent idea you could adapt for other savings projects. Free of charge, the American Girl
Savings Game is well worth a toll-free phone call.
(800) 845-0005.

Endnotes

— $\$$ —

Introduction

1. Third Women's Policy Research Conference Proceedings: Exploring the Quincentennial [Part 43 of 90], *Contemporary Women's Issues Database*, 1 January 1994, 173–76.

2. "After the Money's Gone," *Washington Times*, 21 June 1998, 37.

3. Goodman, Ellen, "The Last Great Sin, Debt, Hits Airwaves," *Newsday*, 11 September 1996, A-39.

Chapter 6

1. Consumer Federation of America.

2. The Associates National Bank of Delaware Visa®.

3. *Ibid.*

4. Robert D. Hershey, Jr., *The New York Times* reported in the *Orange County Register*, "A Method to Avoid the Madness," Monday, 11 November 1996.

5. Alan D. Blair, "A High Wire Act: Balancing Student Loan and Credit Card Debt," Director of Credit Management at Nellie Mae, the largest nonprofit provider of education loan funds in the nation and a major philanthropic contributor to educational programs serving low-income, disadvantaged youth (http://www.nelliemae.com/about/balance.htm/), 1997.

6. Donna Freedman, "Debt-101: Teens Headed for College Find Credit Cards All Too Tempting," *Anchorage Daily News,* 14 May 1998, D-1.

7. Letter from *Cheapskate Monthly* subscriber, Maureen Mushat, Ohio.

8. Letter from *Cheapskate Monthly* subscriber, Cyd Bogner, Ohio.

9. Letter from *Cheapskate Monthly* subscriber, Kay Sabo, Colorado.

10. Letter from *Cheapskate Monthly* subscriber, Cynthia Porter, Ohio.

11. American Student List Company.

12. Bob McKinley, RAM Research Corp., as quoted by Steve Emmons, "Giving Teenagers Credit," *L.A. Times,* 26 June 1993.

13. Letter from *Cheapskate Monthly* subscriber, Sharon Norick, Oregon.

14. Letter from *Cheapskate Monthly* subscriber, Paula Clements, Texas.

15. Lisa McKendall, spokeswoman for Mattel, which is based in El Segundo, CA, posted $1.9 billion in Barbie sales in 1997 and would not disclose the terms of the

deal that allowed Mattel to use the MasterCard name and logo on Barbie's credit card. She would only say that Mattel contacted MasterCard about it. MasterCard did not return phone calls.

16. "Kids, Cash, Plastic, and You," produced by MasterCard International in cooperation with the U.S. Office of Consumer Affairs and the Consumer Information Center.

17. Letter from *Cheapskate Monthly* subscriber, Stephanie Adam, Missouri.

Chapter 7

1. Rand Youth Poll and James U. McNeal, professor of marketing at Texas A&M University.

2. "The Kids Market," Packaged Facts, New York-based research firm, March 1997.

3. "The Teens Market," Packaged Facts, January 1997.

4. *Ibid.*

5. Greg Johnson, "Catalogs Court Shop-Til-You-Drop Teenagers," *Los Angeles Times,* 9 October 1997. D-1.

6. Jane M. Von Bergen, "Generation Y, as in Y not shop and spend?" Knight Ridder Newspapers from Deptford Township, N.J, as reported in the *Orange County Register,* 15 February 1998.

7. Quoted in "Hey Kid, Buy This!" *TV-Free American,* Winter 1997, attributed to the *New York Times,* March 1994.

8. Quoted in "The Kids Market, Executive Summary" survey taken and results published by Packaged Facts,

625 Avenue of the Americas, New York, NY 10011. Quote attributed to *The New York Times,* 8 April 1996.

9. "Hey Kid, Buy This!" *TV-Free America Newsletter,* Winter 1997 issue.

10. S. C. Gwynne, "Hot News in Class," *Time,* 18 December 1995.

11. John Murray, "TV in the Class Room: News or Nikes?" *EXTRA!* Sept.-Oct. 1991.

12. Bradley Greenberg and Jeffrey Brand, "Channel One," *Educational Leadership*, January 1994.

13. "Future Debtors of America," *Consumer Reports,* December 1997, 18.

14. High School Student Consumer Knowledge: A Nationwide Test sponsored by the Consumer Federation of America and American Express Company, results released September 1991.

15. College Student Consumer Knowledge: A Nationwide Test sponsored by Consumer Federation of America and American Express Company, results released September 1993.

16. *CardTrak News,* Ram Research, September 1997, http://www.ramresearch.com.

Chapter 9

1. From *Influence: Science and Practice*, 3rd ed. by Robert B. Cialdini, copyright © 1993 by HarperCollins College Publishers, 78-79. Reprinted by permission of Addison Wesley Educational Publishers Inc.

2. Charles R. Swindoll, *You and Your Child* (Nashville: Thomas Nelson, 1977), 27.

3. Gary Smalley, *The Key to Your Child's Heart* (Dallas: Word, 1996), 49-52.

4. Swindoll, 27.

Chapter 11

1. Alvin Danenberg, *21 1/2 Easy Steps to Financial Security* (Chicago: International Publishing, 1995), 50.

What Is *Cheapskate Monthly*?

– $$$ –

Cheapskate Monthly is a 12-page newsletter published 12 times a year, dedicated to helping those who are struggling to live within their means find practical and realistic solutions to their financial problems. *Cheapskate Monthly* provides hope, encouragement, inspiration, and motivation to individuals who are committed to financially responsible and debt-free living and provides the highest-quality information and resources possible in a format exclusive of paid advertising. You will find *Cheapskate Monthly* filled with tips, humor, and great information to help you stretch those dollars till they scream!

Special Offer from *Cheapskate Monthly*

How to Subscribe to *Cheapskate Monthly*

Send check or money order for $18.00 to:
Cheapskate Monthly
P.O. Box 2135
Paramount, CA 90723-8135
(562) 630-8845 for information only
(800) 550-3502 for phone orders only
http://www.cheapskatemonthly.com
(Please call for Canadian and foreign rates)

Special Offer

Enclose this original coupon with your check or money order, and your one-year subscription to *Cheapskate Monthly* will be automatically extended for an additional three months. That's 15 months for the price of 12. Such a deal, considering $18.00 for 12 full issues is already CHEAP!!

(Subscription rate subject to change without notice.)

More great resources for
DEBT-FREE LIVING

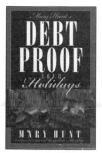

DEBT PROOF YOUR HOLIDAYS

Every year, just like clockwork, come the holidays. And every year most of us overspend. But this year can be different, thanks to America's favorite cheapskate. Mary Hunt gives advice on enjoying the holidays in a way that won't create January mail anxiety. With hundreds of ideas for everything from gifts to decorating, *Debt Proof Your Holidays* is the best spent $8.99 of the season!

Trade Paper 0-8054-1678-1

THE COMPLETE CHEAPSKATE

You can save money and still have fun! Mary Hunt offers practical advice on saving, using a systematic approach to money management, and spending. After racking up more than $100,000 in credit card debt, Mary turned her life around – and now she invites readers to learn from her mistakes.

Trade Paper 0-8054-1770-2

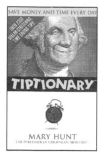

TIPTIONARY

When Mary Hunt talks cheap, everybody listens! America's favorite cheapskate has put together this great collection of tips for living well while within your means. If your life seems to be getting more expensive, more time-consuming, more exhausting, and more frustrating, this is the idea antidote. With creative solutions for saving time and money on everything from gardening to auto repairs, Mary shows how to spend less and enjoy life more, no matter how much – or how little – money a person has.

Trade Paper 0-8054-0147-4

available at fine bookstores everywhere

More great resources for
DEBT-FREE LIVING

THE FINANCIALLY CONFIDENT WOMAN

The Financially Confident Woman tells the story of Mary's journey to the brink of financial disaster and back. She documents the hidden dangers of easy credit, shows women how to control their financial futures, identifies nine characteristics of financially confident women, and offers detailed plans for turning bad financial habits around and putting sound financial principles into action!
Trade Paper 0-8054-6285-6
Audio Book (read by the author) 0-8054-8378-0

THE FINANCIALLY CONFIDENT WOMAN PERPETUAL CALENDAR

0-8054-0008-7

THE FINANCIALLY CONFIDENT WOMAN MINI BOOK

0-8054-6300-3

available at fine bookstores everywhere